Jump Jockeys

An epic steeplechasing picture as King (left) steadies Canasta Lad across the final fence on their way to victory in Cheltenham's Arkle Chase.

Final flight of the Brewers' Hurdle at Doncaster, November 1979. The legs of Pulse Rate (right) buckle and Jonjo O'Neill cannot prevent him leaning into King's mount, Palace Dan. King took the race on an objection.

Alan Lee with Jeff King

Ward Lock Limited · London

© Alan Lee 1980

First published in Great Britain in 1980
by Ward Lock Limited, 47 Marylebone Lane,
London W1M 6AX, a Pentos Company.

House editor Gill Freeman

Text set in Plantin
by Computacomp (UK) Ltd.,
Fort William, Scotland.

Printed in Great Britain by
Hollen Street Press, Slough.

British Library Cataloguing in Publication Data

Lee, Alan
   Jump jockeys.
   1. Jockeys – Great Britain
   2. Steeplechasing
   I. Title   II. King, Jeff
   798'.45'0922   SF336.2

ISBN 0-7063-6064-8

Contents

Introduction

The Breed

I have never ridden a horse, or even wanted to, really. As a boy, I grew up believing horses were for girls, rosettes and gymkhanas; when older, I adopted the cynical view that they belonged only in a world of unshaven, fag-ash characters who spent all their days in dingy betting shops. Racing was an irritation which interrupted the sports I wanted to watch on Saturday afternoon television. Lester Piggot and Scobie Breasley were the only jockeys I had heard of, and I could not even have told you if they rode on the flat or over jumps. It was all the same to me—and pretty tedious at that.

Becoming a sports writer did little to change my ways. Something of a sport apart, racing rarely requires the services of any but its own specialist reporters and in my first ten years of journalism I wrote not a single word about it, and was thankful.

It is difficult to reconstruct what happened then. I attended a winter race meeting or two, with friends and found myself developing a fascination for the job of the jockey or, to be more precise, the jump jockey. To this day, I have managed to generate little enthusiasm for flat racing—a bloodless sprint which is over while you blink and appears to demand little of its jockeys—but the jumping game has hooked me. I may still know little about the horses themselves, but to be frank I follow them far less avidly than the characters on board, the men who provide a richer tapestry of personalities than any other sport I have encountered.

Looking at it from a distance and viewing with simplistic understatement, the jump jockey breed can be generalised in various categories: they are all relatively small, they are sociable creatures who work unsocial hours, they are courageous but never boastful, smart but rarely flash. They share a like humour and an individual language which can sometimes baffle the outsider. They drive upwards of 50,000 miles a season, suffer an average of one fall in ten rides and one serious injury a year. The successful make enough money to live comfortably, though never spectacularly; the remainder struggle.

The characters, however, are as varied as the conditions they must work in—although the hard-bitten, frosty type is close to extinction.

Not one jockey refused to co-operate with this project; not one mocked me for my confessed naivety; not one, and here is the most striking fact in these days of sporting mercenaries, asked for money. For most, it seemed that the satisfaction of knowing that their vastly underexposed profession was to receive some publicity was ample reward.

My idea was to chart the movements, incidents and emotions in one jockey's season, but having set off with that intention, the approachability of each rider expanded the story into a more general look at the lifestyle of these sportsmen. There are, however, hundreds of licenced jump jockeys, scores of good ones and dozens with something interesting to say. It was not feasible to talk to them all, and practicability dictated that much of my circuit was confined to the south.

National Hunt jockeys divide themselves geographically, an economically sound step considering they pay all their own travelling expenses. The north–south distinction is a loose one, as there will be various occasions during a season when a southern jockey takes rides at a northern meeting, and *vice versa*, while the midland tracks remain common ground. It is generally accepted that there are less top-class jockeys in the north, which often means that their stars—Jonjo O'Neill, Tommy Carmody, Ron Barry and Ridley Lamb—will ride five or six times at one meeting whereas the southern riders, faced with keener competition, have to be satisfied with a general maximum of three or four.

The job does not begin and end at the races, however. Those jockeys who are attached to a stable—paid a retainer to ride all the horses trained there—are expected to work most mornings, too, 'riding out' the horses either for gallops or on the roads. Freelance riders are also engaged by trainers, both for riding out and schooling their horses over fences. In both cases, the rider generally works without payment, his only reward being the intangible hope that he will have a few quid on the way from race-riding for that trainer.

As an existence, it is more perilous than most. Some companies will insure a jump jockey against the daily dangers he meets, but in the event of an injury, he relies heavily on the goodwill of the Injured Jockeys' Fund. Even when fit, there are no guarantees of regular employment for the vast majority of freelances. Get in a good run, ride a few winners, and the phone will scarcely stop ringing with offers from trainers. Upset an owner, or simply go a few weeks without a winner, and you can begin to wonder where the next ride is coming from. Loyalty is a rare commodity in modern sport, and as difficult to find in steeplechasing as anywhere else; just because you have been riding for a certain trainer for ten years, you cannot afford to bank on his business again in the future.

Even those who are retained by a trainer will not grow rich on it. In jump racing, £2,000 a season is a good retainer—yet it represents a pittance when compared to the five-figure amounts paid to flat jockeys for similar services.

The distinction, jumping and flat, poor and rich, is a paradox, as National Hunt undoubtedly provides a far better spectacle for its watchers, yet attracts relatively little in the way of prize money and virtually nothing in individual sponsorship and advertising.

The Jockey Club, for reasons that presumably they alone understand, cling to the primitive notion that it is wrong for employees to exploit their popularity, success, good looks or personality for gain. So, a year or two ago, they vetoed a bid by Graham Thorner, now retired, to wear an advertising insignia on his jockey breeches. More recently, John Francome, enterprising and much in demand, has experimented by wearing his initials all down the seam of his breeches, partly to gauge the effect on television, chiefly to see if commercial companies would be sufficiently attracted.

Jonjo O'Neill, champion twice in the last three seasons, has a commercial agent—yet, like almost every one of his colleagues, his face remains virtually unknown to the general public despite the fact that he appears on television every Saturday through the season.

Things may eventually change and perhaps, just like cricketers, whose potential rewards doubled almost overnight, jump jockeys will ultimately be paid what they are worth. In the meantime, they receive £32 for each ride—the new figure, increased last season—and ten per cent of the winner's prize money for each horse they get home first. Out of that, they pay their own expenses, including a fee for the services of a valet.

It would be wrong to infer that all jump jockeys live on the breadline in suburban slums. Many, indeed, have enviable properties. But many more are forced to quit simply because they could not live on the money they are earning.

The risks are well chronicled, but perhaps they bear repeating here. If a jockey, for instance, rides in two steeplechases and two hurdle races in one afternoon, it is likely that he will travel about ten miles on horseback—barring falls—and tackle something like 50 obstacles, any one of which could put him in hospital. It is rare for any jockey to survive a season without some sort of injury break but few, thankfully, are as unfortunate as the tragic Jonathan Haynes, whose riding life ended soon after his 20th birthday when he was dragged out from under his fallen horse, paralysed from the chest down.

Just occasionally, however, more danger is provided by human interference than fences and a jockey's sense of humour is at a premium in situations like one described by Philip Blacker, Stan Mellor's number one rider:

'We jumped off at Uttoxeter one day, and coming to the second fence we saw a man standing in front of it. There was a lot of yelling and shouting and he scampered out of the way just in time. We completed the circuit and approached the same fence again. I couldn't believe my eyes. The same bloke was sitting on the rail of the fence, eating his sandwiches! When he heard us yelling again, he leaped to his feet and just froze, right in the middle of the fence. The field had to divide and jump around him.'

Blacker's tale is one of the best, but by no means unique. John Francome tells a similar story of a thoughtless spectator caught in front of a fence. His solution was to jump into the open ditch.

Humour is a bond between jump jockeys. It is there in every weighing-room, where the riders change before racing, it is there on the course itself, and it is there in abundance in the bars and pubs afterwards. They are a funny breed, in the nicest sense of the phrase.

When they talk racing, a stickler for grammar would continually interject with corrections. The present tense, oddly, is almost always substituted for the future; instead of saying 'I will be riding at Ascot on Saturday' the phraseology is 'I ride at Ascot ...' and so on. There are any number of other catch-phrases, peculiar to those in the game and peculiar (in the other sense) to those who are not. For instance, a horse with a slight chance in any race *has a squeak*, a horse jumping a fence well has *pinged it*, and a horse which has not been trying on a trainer's orders—in other words, has been stopped—is *not off*. It took me a long while to translate them all and there are still times now when I stand silent in complete bafflement.

At the races, jockeys tend to wear a collar and tie. There are no hard and fast rules about dress, but almost without exception, they conform to a pattern. Open-neck shirts, or roll-neck sweaters, are worn at mid-week country meetings—on tracks, incidentally, known as *gaffs*—but suits, or jackets are almost universally accepted for the bigger meetings.

Certain jockeys do develop superstitions. Young Steve Knight, second jockey to trainer Bob Turnell, was enjoying a magnificent run towards the end of the season and earned himself almost £10,000 in prize money in the space of a month. Because the run had begun where he wore a brown, three-piece suit to a meeting, he wore the same suit on every race-day thereafter.

Richard Evans, a Midlands freelance, believes in a different formula.

'I was looking through the form, one day during a lean time, and noticed that most of the successful jockeys used two initials—T. W. Biddlecombe, B. R. Davies and so on. It seemed to me that plain R. Evans was too easy to overlook, so I added another initial in the hope of my name being noticed by more owners and trainers. Ever since then, I've been R. R. Evans.'

To many flat jockeys, the mere mention of the words 'food and drink' are enough to produce a rush to the bathroom scales and a feverish check to see if an ounce has slipped on somewhere. Jump jockeys, in general, have fewer weight problems. The minimum they are ever required to be is 10 stone, and there are many who permanently ride well above that figure. Francome, for instance, seldom gets below 10st. 6lbs., yet he is one of the few who have fought a lengthy, exasperating and sometimes unhealthily strict battle against the pounds. His diet allows him few luxuries, yet I take with me from the season the memory of him loading his car with no less than six different chocolate bars for a journey home from Nottingham.

Francome, incidentally, is abstemious about alcohol too, but that has only a coincidental benefit to his diet. He simply does not like the stuff—nor, apparently, does it like him. One half pint of lager and lime in a Cotswold pub one Saturday evening, and he declared he was 'staggering' on the way to the door.

In that regard, however, both Francome and the tee-total O'Neill are exceptions to the jump jockey rule. Most see drinking as part of social life, and social life as part of the job. There have, I am confidently informed, been countless occasions of winners being ridden by jockeys who were incapable with drink only hours before.

In a profession which demands a high degree of dedication, however, such excesses can be forgiven. An escape outlet sometimes has to be found, and the sociability of the apré race gatherings are undoubtedly a good method of winding-down. Golf is favoured by some as a spare-time and Sunday pursuit, and a number of jump jockeys are also keen cricketers, as is evidenced by the existence of their own team, whose annual dinner in February was an occasion of bawdy revelry among the limps, crutches and black eyes of the day's racing.

A wide spectrum of social backgrounds allows no generalisation in jockey's politics—although it would be fair to say most are happier with a Tory rule—reading or music preferences.

Just as I saw examples of jockeys taking *The Times*, the *Sun* and everything in between, along with the inevitable *Sporting Life*, so musical tastes vary between Francome's love of contemporary rock and O'Neill's liking for Irish country songs.

They are, however, all much the same in certain respects. They all appear to love animals, from the essential horses to dogs, cats and other pets; they all drink tea in the weighing-room as well as at home; and they all seem to drive cars fast, perhaps as a sub-conscious reaction to their enormous seasonal mileage.

They all love winning. But few love it more than the job.

The Man—Jeff King

Jeff King came into the world in the year that the little matter of repelling the Third Reich began to occupy Britons to such an unthinkable degree that the Grand National was abandoned for the first time in 105 years. Despite this handicap, as soon as he was old enough to think King was determined to be a jockey, and practised his techniques endlessly, riding on the back of his uncle Reg near the family home in Exeter.

King was actually born in the village of Shaldon, on the mouth of the River Teign and a short drive from Newton Abbot racecourse. He never thought much of schoolwork and, like so many who find their way into the racing game, left at the first opportunity to be with horses.

He was apprenticed to Sir Gordon Richards at Marlborough, and he now lives nearby, with wife Maureen and children David and Helen. Flat racing provided King with few rides and no winners, but when his weight increased to an impossible level, he transferred his developing skills to National Hunt.

For 13 years, he was stable jockey to Bob Turnell, much of the time sharing the rides with his friend Johnny Haine, now a modestly successful trainer. But when Turnell's son Andy grew to riding age, the stable became a family affair and King lost the job he had loved.

He rode as retained jockey to Peter Bailey for several years, but latterly has been completely freelance. In 1980, he celebrated 21 years in jump-racing, considerably longer than any other current jockey.

In planning this book, I looked as collaborator for a jockey with much experience but limited glories. I wanted a man who would talk honestly and revealingly about his job to someone who was viewing it as a total outsider. Everyone I asked mentioned the name of Jeff King. He is honest, I was warned, to the point of being decidedly blunt and, so they all said, it has not always furthered his career. But in the saddle, there are none better.

John Francome, the man who King himself now rates as the country's best jockey, says of him: 'If I had Jeff's ability, I would wonder why I hadn't been champion three or four times.' Richard Evans, the epitome of the steady, reliable professional, suggests: 'Kingy is three jockeys in one—the best I have ever seen'. Jonjo O'Neill calls him 'the last man I want to see upsides me in a finish' and Lord Oaksey, respected commentator and once a successful amateur, says 'He has my idea of the best method in anyone riding today.'

King also has his detractors, I discovered. As a man with strong views about most things in racing, he has inevitably suffered clashes of opinion and personality throughout his long career. It still occurs today, and there are owners and trainers who would go out of their way to avoid putting him up on their horses.

But neither lavish praise nor damning criticism visibly affect King. He is a quiet and deep man, who keeps emotions in check and thoughts under cover. If he has survived two decades in the top bracket of jump jockeys, he reasons, he cannot have upset too many people in power and, while one can sense an inner frustration at his failure to land any of the most major honours, it is a feeling tempered with acceptance of a lot

Bob Turnell, King's employer for 13 years, seemingly lost in thought as he discusses his victory on The Laird in the 1967 Stones Ginger Wine Chase at Sandown Park.

Indianapolis (far right) clears the final flight at Newbury to give King one of his most prestigious wins, in the 1973 Schweppes Gold Trophy.

TOP: King (centre) drives home the grey, Tudor Legend, in the Liverpool Hurdle at Aintree.

ABOVE: Roman Holiday, perhaps King's favourite horse among all he has ridden, in classic jumping pose in 1975, when he was a mere 12 years old.

that is by no means a bad one by the standards of his sport.

King owns a house overlooking Marlborough Downs, and 40 acres of land go with it, all the result of a shrewd investment some years ago. A dozen stable boxes take up one corner and are used for a livery business run by his friend, Bill Shoemark. The shell of a high-roofed building stands waiting for completion—the indoor riding school which could occupy part of King's time when he decides to finish racing. A few cows roam the fields attached, and King frequently spends hours out there in his tractor, every inch the gentleman farmer.

On race days, he is generally up soon after seven, and as breakfast rarely interests him, spends the early part of the morning riding out for Shoemark. Then he will soak in the bath and change into racing clothes—in most cases a suit and always something smart—before setting off for the course of the day.

King hates driving and, whenever possible, he will hand over the controls of his Peugeot to someone else. Like most jockeys, he will travel many miles a season and, just occasionally, will take in two meetings in one day—such as the Saturday in mid-April this year when he rode in the 2.15 p.m. at Stratford, then raced across country for a mount in the 4.45 p.m. at Huntingdon. Neither horse won, and he had to leave Stratford with the result of a stewards' enquiry involving his horse, which was third, still not known.

No jockey is entirely nerveless and King confesses he is often keyed up for big races. 'There is perhaps a fear of failure involved, but never a fear of injury. If that day came, it would be time to give up. I have seen a number of jump jockeys lose their nerve, maybe after a bad fall or a succession of them, and the only sensible thing to do then is quit.'

Superstitions in racing tend to fall into patterns, and King fits them. 'I would never have a green car,' he says, 'as that is supposed to be unlucky in racing. And I always say good morning to magpies.' These quirks apart, his only faithful routine is putting on his left boot first before riding.

A great believer in the social side of racing, as a means of winding down as well as an enjoyment, King sometimes drinks beer, more often vodka and tonic and occasionally—when wasting to meet a weight—white wine. He smokes, up to a maximum of 20 a day, reached chiefly on race days when car journeys and pub stops provide the cue for a cigarette or two.

At home, Jeff frequents two pubs in the Wiltshire village of Broad Hinton and is known by all the regulars. He plays dominoes with the locals most Tuesday evenings, but by far his favourite relaxation is golf.

Playing off a handicap of 14, King is a more than average club player and enjoys two or three games a week during his off-season in the summer. He used to play cricket regularly, but his appearances are rare since the days of the breathalyser.

Although the jockey's life carries unusual hours, Jeff is a gentle and attentive family man, but in no hurry to push his son into following father's footsteps. David's interest in horses, sometimes keen, is at present no more than spasmodic and King is perfectly content to leave him free to choose his own career.

Maureen works part-time for a book club, plays bridge regularly and to a high standard, and comes racing once a year, to Liverpool for the Grand National. She is not encouraged to make more frequent trips as King, like many other jockeys, is never completely at ease with her watching. 'I don't like the idea of her seeing me get hurt. If it happens, she will know about it soon enough, without the anguish of wondering how serious it might be.'

'Racing is my work,' he points out. 'If I worked in a factory, I would not take my wife there with me.'

On the rare occasions that Maureen has appeared outside the Aintree meeting, things have normally gone wrong. She recalls that she went to Cheltenham on the day that Jeff rode The Laird in the Gold Cup. 'He was rated a near-certainty to win,' she says. 'But he fell, and when I met Jeff afterwards he was sullen and speechless. By the time he had got over it enough to talk, I was in such a mood that I wasn't speaking to him.'

Jeff rarely talks racing at home, and Maureen seldom questions him about it. She is, however, far from insensitive to his changing fortunes and subsequently changing moods. 'It's time he rode a winner,' she told me one day. 'He hasn't said a word about it, but I know he is worried.'

The jump jockey's life is full of peaks and troughs. The winners tend to arrive in floods but in the bad times of falls and losers, nobody wants to know you. But if life began again, Jeff King for one would order the same all round.

The Stars

Jockeys are different from the majority of individual sportsmen in that they can never entirely be judged on results. It does not matter how good the man on top may be at his job, if the horse is useless the partnership has no chance of winning.

Similarly, although it is common to hear the trite remark that a certain jockey is either in good form or bad, simple logic dictates the foolishness of the statement. Once he has the ability and the courage, a jump jockey does not run in and out of form. Indeed, unless he suffers a complete loss of nerve or confidence, his results are chiefly due to the quality of the horses beneath him.

There are obviously, however, good jockeys and bad, those with style and those without, and there are few people better qualified to judge such standards than Jeff King.

King does not adhere to the perennial complaint of old-stagers that things ain't what they used to be. 'I hear many trainers say there are no good riders around these days, but it just isn't true. Because there are many more jockeys than when I began riding, it is logical that there are more bads ones about. But I do not believe the standard at the top has dropped.'

Ridley Lamb, Steven Smith-Eccles, Paul Barton, Paul Leach, Richard Evans, Graham McCourt, David Goulding, Steve Knight, Hywel Davies, Richard Rowe and Christy Kinane are all commended by King as capable pilots, but six of his current contemporaries stand out.

John Francome 'My idea of the most complete jump jockey in the business. He is better than Jonjo O'Neill, his major rival, in the country, and is the best I have ever seen at the obstacles. John's talents come down to superb horsemanship, and the fact that he was a junior international showjumper before coming into racing must have helped him in terms of judging stride. John was never apprenticed, nor did he ride on the flat. Indeed, as he was about 17 before he began riding at all, his development is quite remarkable. A few years ago, one could point to his finishing as a weak point, but he has worked so hard at it that I would now rate him as strong as anyone at the business end of a race. He is one of the prime jokers in the weighing-room and a very cool character at all times.'

Jonjo O'Neill 'A very good champion and probably the most dedicated jump jockey I have ever known. Jonjo drives more miles, and spends more time with the job than anyone else riding today, so deserves all the success he has had on that pretext alone. He is also, however, very strong, a good race-rider in terms of judging pace and position, and pretty good at the obstacles. As he has always been based in the north, I saw little of Jonjo in his formative years as a jockey, but he certainly got going in the game very quickly, and never stopped riding more and more winners from the time he left Gordon Richards' stable to go freelance. Jonjo is often accused of being stick-happy, and I would agree that in 1978, when he first won the title, and the following year, he did use his whip too much. He appeared to get carried away to the extent that every horse he rode just had to win. This past season, he has been nowhere near as severe. As a personality, Jonjo is smashing—just because he does not drink, there is no reason for thinking him a misery. He loves a joke in the weighing-room and seems to wear a permanent smile.'

Tommy Carmody 'A very different type of jockey from both Francome and O'Neill, Tommy rides very short which, to my mind, cannot possibly be an advantage to a jump jockey. It is a habit he picked up when riding on the flat and, since he has been successful, he is understandably reluctant to change. Tommy is a very competent race-rider with a good deal of flair and cheek. He judges a race well and, although a good many of his rides are front-running types, he can also drop one in nicely. He emerged on the scene very rapidly 18 months ago and has had two fine seasons. I tend to see little of him socially as, again, he lives and rides in the north, but he is a cheerful character in the weighing-room.'

Andy Turnell   'Rides as short as Carmody which, again, is why he is not my type of jockey. But Andy does have tremendous ability, and is renowned for his talent in judging pace and playing the waiting game. He was better to watch when he rode longer, some years ago; I watched Andy grow up, through riding for his father, and he always thought Lester Piggott was out of this world. It may have been that which influenced his decision to ride short, but it began when he injured his leg and it felt more comfortable that way. A quiet man in the weighing-room these days, Andy is essentially a gentle, sensitive rider, which is why the allegations of excessive use of the whip, made against him at Cheltenham and Liverpool, were so startling.'

Ron Barry   'Known to everyone as "Big Ron" in a weighing-room currently very short on nicknames, he has been riding since 1964 and has been champion jockey twice. Based in the north-west corner of England, Ron generally travels with Jonjo, which is slightly ironical as they have alternated as stable jockey to Gordon Richards for some years. Ron, who now holds the job since Jonjo has gone freelance, is a tremendously strong rider with a great ability to make horses jump for him. He is now married with children, but has always been one to enjoy the social life of the profession and is great fun to have around.'

Bob Davies   'Retained by Bury St Edmonds trainer David Morley, Bob is among the quietest and most sympathetic of jockeys, and has been in the top bracket for many years now. Champion jockey three times, he has always achieved a consistently high number of winners. A chatty and amiable man, he is by no means among the more boisterous of riders. Bob is one of the few jump jockeys with a university degree behind him and, by combining his riding skills with such a good brain, he has looked after his future very soundly.'

1 Fog and frustration

Chepstow

With a single slap from his stick, Jeff King brought Doddington Park smoothly away from the final fence, held off the favourite by three lengths and claimed his seventh win of the season with about as much elation as I was beginning to expect from him. Absolutely none.

After 21 years as a jump jockey, he wore the unsmiling, almost grim mask in the saddle as a permanent arrangement. Something special was needed to crack those features and a winner in the 1.45 at Chepstow was not that certain something.

It was not the sort of day to inspire high emotion. All down the M4 from his home near Swindon, the weather had pronounced that winter was with us a little early this year. Fog still hung over the downs, flurries of rain decorated the windscreen. Snow was forecast. The River Severn looked bleak and dirty as gusty winds played games with King's car, but we were barely past the bi-lingual sign bidding us 'Welcome to Wales' when an impressive set of stone gates topped by a pair of sculptured lions from warmer climes beckoned us into Chepstow racecourse. Our arrival coincided with a helicopter, landing one of the prosperous owners in the centre of the course, and a couple of seasoned racing buffs wearing the red noses and purposeful gazes which suggested a warming whisky or two before the first.

King, clutching a bundle of riding tack under each arm, disappeared into the jockey's shrine—the weighing-room, above which a bold notice insists that even owners and trainers are forbidden to set foot inside. There was an hour to kill before the first race, and the place was hardly buzzing with anticipation. Gatemen, shivering and stamping in the fine drizzle, guarded every members' entrance and virtually outnumbered the early punters. The bookies were still setting up their stalls in the ring, observed by a handful of impatient gamblers, and in the members' bar—a glass-fronted room fitted snugly under the stewards' viewing balcony—the chatter was not encouraging.

A short way removed from the cluster of predictable sheepskins and flat caps sat two fascinating ladies, sixtyish and dressed remarkably similarly in cardigans, roll-neck sweaters, tweed skirts, knitted woollen stockings and fur ankle-boots. Over hot soup and pasties, they discussed one of what must have been countless previous racing days together then, in unison, consulted the day's card and turned up their noses. 'Awful racing today, dear,' one sniffed. What is more, they were right. The scheduled six-race programme had been reduced to five as only one horse remained entered for the last—'disgraceful', said King—and, of the rest, one was for amateur jockeys only and another had only three runners.

King was to ride only once, in what was undoubtedly the best-class race of the day. Only six runners, but mostly competent horses and, of these, three, including Doddington Park, were strongly fancied.

The windows of the bar started to steam up as more refugees from the damp outside burst in and the colour television began to show the day's racing from three other meetings—Chepstow, significantly, was the one course of the day not favoured with the cameras. A solitary girl dressed for Ascot high summer looked oddly conspicuous. The pasty pile shrank fast and the coffee sales were rivalling those of medicinal brandy.

As if by some unheard call, the bar emptied ten minutes before the first race, won comfortably by the favourite, and then filled again for further consultation of race-cards and another spell in front of the telly, which was now—rather chillingly—cheerfully running some snowy, Christmas commercials.

Outside, the bookies had installed Doddington Park as 5 to 4 favourite, but that didn't last long. Directed by the magical language of the tick-tack men, the odds lengthened. Soon, King's mount was 2 to 1 and by the time the gate went up, the bookies had softened to 11 to 4 and rated two other horses ahead of him.

The parade ring at Chepstow lies behind the members' stand. After five minutes of circling by their mounts, the jockeys emerged. King, frowning slightly and with his arms crossed against the cold, entered the ring in sky blue garb and waited for the ritual to begin.

The owners were released into the ring and made an elegant stampede for their respective jockey and trainer. King and Doddington Park's trainer Nick Gaselee were almost engulfed by half-a-dozen eager-looking folk, all of whom apparently had a stake—known as a 'leg'—in the horse. King respectfully touched his cap to the ladies, nodded to the men and shared the briefest of tactical talks with Gaselee before the call to mount took him gratefully away from the frozen huddle.

It was a two-mile steeplechase and King led from the start. 'He's a free running horse who always pulls hard until he is over the first,' he explained later. 'With novices, there is no point in fighting to steady them so I let him do as he pleased in the early stages.' A grey called Dutchman galloped stride for stride with Doddington Park for half the long, hilly circuit, then fell four fences from home. The rest was easy—

or at least, that was how it looked to my untrained eye in the stand.

At the last fence, Spring Frolic—ominously for others, trained by Fred Winter—came to challenge, but with that one, nominal crack from his whip, King hastened his mount into an unassailable lead. He returned to the winners' enclosure with one hand on the reins, the other resting a little tiredly on his thigh, dismounted and instantly began to examine a fore-leg. Gaselee joined him, then the owners, and soon there were six pairs of eyes staring at a minor rip in the skin. It might be tendon trouble, it might not, but even before King had returned to the weighing-room, Gaselee was pessimistically predicting a six-week break for the horse.

King changed, accepted the owners' invitation to a drink and returned to the stand to watch the remaining races. Only after the last, when sharing the bar-space with a few friends, did the face crack and the humorous side of King appear. Talk ranged back over the years, to horses and races long gone. But this was November 17, 1979 and Jeff King, in his 39th year, was still riding ... a star with other jockeys if not with the record books.

No other jockey in the country had been riding so long. King was the senior professional, highly respected among the racing fraternity yet no celebrity among any other group. He had never been champion jockey and had won neither the Grand National nor the Cheltenham Gold Cup.

What he had done was spend most of his life riding horses around most of England's racecourses in weather of every conceivable description. The majority, naturally, did not win; some did not even complete the course. King, despite his claims that he has been lucky with injury, has broken leg, collarbone, ribs and pelvis, and fractured his skull—all from National Hunt racing.

He had seen more depressing days in the rain than any other jockey alive—but had also tasted as many moments of sweet exhilaration as most. Chepstow, cold and wet on November 17, was nothing new to Jeff King. He had seen it all before.

Kempton

Four days later, and 30 miles closer to London, another of National Hunt racing's unfriendly aspects had its say. Fog, sweeping along the Thames Valley and loitering over the lakes of Sunbury, enveloped the Kempton Park course and made a farce of the day's sport.

There is something ludicrous about the sight of several hundred people, otherwise sane and upstanding, shivering on cold terrace steps and straining their eyes hopelessly into a massed blanket of nothingness. Like blind men waiting for their sight to return, they suffered in silence as their money disappeared into the murk, then stamped their feet and smiled thinly at the absurdity of it all until, two minutes later, dark forms emerged half-way down the straight. The horses, on average, were in sight from the stand for 56 seconds in each two-mile race; silence reigned uneasily until the race-caller, who can seldom have had a less exacting day, picked out the leader five yards short of the final flight. The frustrations of the long, dark wait then exploded in a roar from those whose money was in the right place and a less healthy sound from those all too dramatically aware that their pounds were only swelling the bookies' wallets.

As an exercise in racing devotion, it was a resounding success. A remarkably good crowd saw it out with a minimum of grumbling until, as the fog thickened visibly after the fourth race, the stewards accepted defeat and abandoned the rest of the programme.

If the experience was a maddening one for the punters, it was hardly a joy for the jockeys. Quite apart from the eerie absence of atmosphere, a depressant to every professional sportsman as much as it is to a cabaret comedian, there was a natural dismay, both about the extra hazards imposed by fog and about the good rides lost.

Jeff King, for instance, accepted with a resignation, born of experience, the fact that his only genuine winning chance in four rides was claimed by the elements. Bird's Custard, strongly fancied for the day's last race, did not get as far as the parade ring and King was left to mull over three distinctly unproductive rides.

The first, Luz Bay, was having his first run over hurdles after an erratic career on the flat. Trailing in towards the rear of a 22-strong novices field, King condemned the horse as 'thoroughly ingenuine'.

Irish Shamrock, sixth of seven in a three-mile chase, had not run for 20 months and King's verdict was: 'He could be OK at a small, country meeting.' The third ride was 'a disappointment'. Although Venture to Cognac was an almost unbackable favourite, King believed his mount, Taikun, could run second. Instead, beset by jangling nerves and jumping abysmally, the horse was pulled up three fences from home. 'I could have pushed on and tried for third place, but there was every chance he would have landed on his back. There was no point in taking the risk.'

Riding in fog, as King explained, is no picnic. 'Today, we could always just about make out the next fence, so it was rideable ... but only just. I have known fog worse than this in which the horses become really frightened. They duck and weave as they approach fences and are quite obviously bewildered by it. Even for the riders, it is a very odd, dreamlike sensation. The jumps are upon you far quicker than you expect and you often have to drag the horse over it. You find that most jockeys look after themselves and ride at a sensible pace. If they didn't, there could be some dreadful pile-ups in this weather.'

It had been a bad day. Three poor rides and one frustration. Cold, damp weather. A wretched drive home, almost blind, to follow. Great game, this jump racing ... I was learning fast that the glamour of the jockey's life is not even skin deep.

Taunton

Richard Evans began race-riding, as an amateur, in 1963, and, for several years past, has been highly rated by the jockeys themselves. He remains, however, an example of one who has rarely been in the right place—or, perhaps, on the right horse—at the right time.

The lucrative and productive retainers have not come his way; he has never challenged in the jockeys' championship; he has never ridden a winner in any of the jumping classics. In his own words, he is 'a middle-of-the-road rider'.

With a family farm, opposite his own home in Stratford-upon-Avon, and the incentive of establishing a horse-stud, Evans is in no hurry to discard what has become 'my way of life rather than my job'. He is a friendly, conversational man with an infectious laugh and that premature, slight stoop which affects so many jockeys. His own shortage of success and exposure does not visibly worry him, and he even managed to chuckle when the occasional futility of his peculiar profession mocked him cruelly at Taunton on December 6.

Evans was not named on the race-card, but had picked up a 'spare ride' on a horse called Clear Deal in a two-mile Novice Chase. Placed twice previously in the season, it was moderately fancied—enough to persuade me to a mild flutter. My money, and Evans' only hope for the day, failed to get as far as the first fence.

Clear Deal, a notorious misbehaver as I discovered too much later, swung round at the start, leaving Evans 20 yards adrift of the field. 'That was bad enough,' he related afterwards, 'but when I did get him going, he threw his head sideways and refused to jump the first.' Left with no alternative, Evans trotted the reluctant mount back to the unsaddling enclosure while the race continued without him. He then changed and went home again. A round-trip of 250 miles, and not a single cleared fence to show for it.

In the first race of that same Taunton meeting, Jeff King had brought a 14 to 1 outsider called Tidal Wave through the field on the long, uphill finishing straight to claim second place. As he turned to canter back and unsaddle, an elderly Somerset wag leaned over the rail and called out: 'Bad luck, Jeff. The bloody thing nearly won, too, when you didn't want him to!'

The barbed insult brought only a wide smile from King, but, as he pointed out later, finishing second in such a race can produce mixed feelings in those connected with a horse. 'I feel Tidal Wave can win his next race, probably over a longer trip,' he explained. 'But after this run, he won't start at a very attractive price and the owner or trainer will not stand to win so much if they fancy a punt.'

2 Falls and fears

The Hennessy

The old fellow selling 'The Sporting Life' in the car-park at Newbury stopped me as I passed him just before mid-day on November 24. 'Fighting Fit's the one to back today, sir', he confided ... and he was right.

This free tip was delivered with a supreme confidence in direct contrast with the moods of the 16 jockeys who were, at that moment, beginning to gather in the weighing-room for the 21st running of the Hennessy Cognac Gold Cup. So much can happen in a race of $3^1/_4$ miles over fences upwards of 4ft. 6in. in height. There is no room for premature bragging; any that could be heard was either nervous bravado or tongue-in-cheek psychology.

The Hennessy is among the half-dozen top jumping races each season, both in terms of prestige and cash reward. It is traditionally run at Newbury on the last Saturday of November and this year, as usual, it was an event which drew a huge crowd, delighting in a rare day of dazzling sunshine.

Racing began at one o'clock, but by noon, most of the jockeys were filing into their changing-rooms. These lead off the main weighing-room and at Newbury, as at most other courses, there are two dressing-rooms, with one valet responsible for each. A valet's duties fall somewhere between those of a laundryman, nursemaid, psychiatrist and father-confessor; in short, he is there to make sure that the jockeys in his care have to do little more than put on the right colours—which he will have laid out anyway—and get on the right horse—over which he has no control! At Newbury, the busy man in overalls with an armful of saddles looked familiar. He was John Buckingham, the man who steered Foinavon through the carnage at the 23rd fence in 1967 to become one of the most famous—and, at 100 to 1, longest-priced— Grand National winners of all time. He was philosophical about his new standing in racing: 'I've been doing it since I gave up riding in 1971,' he said. 'I see a lot of sights, hear a lot of gossip—but I reckon, if you don't mind hard work, it's not a bad life.'

By 12.30, those sights and gossips were multiplying fast. The colour television in the jockey's cosy, adjoining tea-bar had graduated from

Noel Edmonds to Grandstand and a handful of riders wandered in for a peep, surreptitiously consulting the amiable Scot behind the counter over their eating requirements. Without fail, they all said: 'I shouldn't really have anything at all, but half a slice of ham in bread won't do any harm, will it?'

The weight worries continued next door, where the unofficial 'practice' scales were in frequent use by this time, as jockeys in the first race experimented with heavier and lighter saddles to meet their stipulated weight. John Buckingham, I noticed, was by now giving the impression of being in six places at once.

Saddles and riding tack were heaped on each peg around three walls of the room, the clearest identification that these were jockeys and not competitors in any other sport. But there were other signs which left a deeper impression. Teeth and tights, for instance.

Around the room, riders were carefully removing false teeth before their race, leaving the cavities glaring like jockey's birthmarks. Most of them, by this stage, were also wearing the sort of nylon tights that I had previously seen only on girls and, just occasionally, soccer goalkeepers. The idea is to give them greater insulation against some of the cruel weather they must face and, once over the initial shock, it does seem a good idea. Slightly incongruous, nonetheless, to watch them sitting around in this undeniably feminine garb while swapping undeniably sordid sex stories.

The old hands, Jeff King and Ron Barry, were parked together in one corner, occasionally joined by Bob Davies, another rider of vast experience who first won the jockey's championship in 1969. The younger riders were left to sort out their own places and one, Philip Blacker, emerged from an apparent trance to tell a dirty joke before changing for his Hennessy ride, 90 minutes early.

King's two mounts for the day were both to carry more than 11 stone, but as he sat on the scales in regular kit and saw them flick just above the 10st. 4lb. mark he shook his head and grimaced. 'I did ten-four comfortably yesterday, but I had a few jars last night and a bit of breakfast this morning,' he said, as if these were frivolous excesses.

John Buckingham managed to grab himself a cup of tea and slice of ham once the jockeys had clumped off for the first, but the bustle was quickly back, and the atmosphere was steadily being charged by the approach of the big race. By 1.45 p.m., 20 minutes before the scheduled off, much of the joviality had diminished.

Steve Smith-Eccles, a rare, double-barrelled northerner, managed to remain as boisterous on his feet as he invariably is in the saddle, as he waited to be reunited with Zongalero, second in last season's Grand National under Bob Davies and, with Smith-Eccles himself, runner-up in two rich chases twelve months ago.

Malcolm Bastard, the lad delegated to the awesome task of replacing injured champion John Francome on Fred Winter's Grand National third, Rough and Tumble, cast frequent nervous glances around him. But over in old lags' corner, Ron Barry still sat with his legs crossed as if waiting for a train, and Bob Davies indulged in some further relaxed chatter.

The floor was littered with unwanted saddles, the air full of good-lucks and the smell of an occasional final fag as the riders finally exited, almost reluctantly and only after four calls from the doorman.

Next door in the tea-bar was the most poignant sight of all. Bob Champion, who had ridden the favourite, Approaching, to victory in the same race a year ago, sat in front of the TV in civilian clothes. Quite what was going on in his mind, one could only guess. Champion had cancer and being a jockey, at least for the present, was out of the question.

Parades are traditional before such major racing events, but the ritual brought the first casualty. Jack Madness, apparently an aptly named horse but under the jockey-trainer partnership of Richard Rowe and Josh Gifford that had already taken the day's first two races, reared dramatically as he came on to the course. Rowe had no chance of staying in the saddle and, by the time he had picked himself up, Jack was half-way across the inside of the course and going strong. No newcomer to this game—he once avoided capture for half-a-day near his home stables—the horse clearly enjoyed making fools of his chasers for slightly more than 20 minutes. When he finally allowed them to win, the stewards had already withdrawn him from the race, unknown to owner, trainer or jockey—none of whom were exactly overjoyed.

Ironically, with one fancied horse already disqualified, the two favourites were then the first to fall—Gaffer at the seventh, Straight Jocelyn at the 12th. Rough and Tumble and young Malcolm Bastard parted company in bone-juddering fashion a fence later and the race resolved itself into a battle up the straight between Fighting Fit and Zongalero. The weight of coincidence dictated that this time, Zongalero must take the prize, but despite all the vigorous driving of Smith-Eccles, the brandy and trophy went to Fighting Fit's Scottish stable ... and opened another line of irony.

Jonjo O'Neill, the Irishman leading the jockey's championship, had been offered the ride on Fighting Fit, but declined. He preferred, in the interests of his title aspirations, to take six fanciable rides at Catterick, on the basis of quantity being more valuable than quality. It is the type of difficult decision that a leading jockey will face more than once during a season, but this time fortune turned cruelly against O'Neill. Not only did Fighting Fit win, with his 'volunteer' replacement Richard Linley on board, but the flu attacked the Irishman and he even had to withdraw from Catterick.

Linley, who had cheekily phoned the Scottish trainer to offer himself

RIGHT: Richard Evans, perennially middle-of-the-road and always, in King's view, a skilful and under-rated horseman.

BELOW: Steve Smith-Eccles' mount, Zongalero, ears pricked, leads over the last in the Hennessy Gold Cup. But it was Fighting Fit, ridden less flamboyantly by Richard Linley, which stayed on better to win.

OVERLEAF: Going and gone ... Gary Moore hits the turf as Winslow Boy comes to grief at Ascot's final fence.

The point of no return for Andy Turnell, catapulting out of the nosediving Secret Ballot's saddle and leaving Lorna Vincent clear to win the SGB Hurdle on Walnut Wonder.

for the ride, now wore the lit-up smile of a schoolboy on prize day. He was rushed from winners' enclosure to weighing-room, then back again to receive a trophy and congratulations and talk to the press. He was still talking, wearing his Hennessy colours, when the order came for the jockeys to mount in the following race. He changed and made it to the start on time, but only just.

Back in the changing-room, Smith-Eccles was slumped on the bench, head forward, beads of sweat running down his face. He was breathing in long, heaving pants and shaking his head continually at the injustice of being forever the bridesmaid. Quite suddenly, he smiled ruefully, and all was comparatively right again. He rode the winner of the fifth race.

Richard Rowe was less consolable. Stripped bare-chested, he prowled into the tea-bar and informed anyone who asked that, with Gaffer and Straight Jocelyn falling, Jack Madness would surely have won. His eyes betrayed the sort of despondency which is always far worse than that which Smith-Eccles was experiencing. To take part and lose really is preferable to not taking part at all and, just at that moment, I had the feeling that Rowe was eyeing a strange hanging contraption in the changing-room which bore a fleeting resemblance to a noose.

Falls and Fears

That Saturday, November 24, was a special day for Jeff King, too. It had nothing to do with the Hennessy, nor even with riding winners—two unproductive mounts at Newbury, in fact, completed a forlorn week of 15 booked rides in which only two were placed and his one outstanding chance of a win was stable-bound by the Kempton fog. But, it had been a year to the day since King suffered the most serious of his countless racing injuries. It had happened on Hennessy day, 1978, when King—without a ride at Newbury—was dispatched to Yorkshire for the meeting which ended his season.

Twelve months on, time had healed the broken leg and clouded his memory on certain facts. He could not recall, for instance, whether his fall came in the second or third race on the Wetherby card, only that it was a $2^1/_2$-mile steeplechase. But the incident itself is still clearly marked on his mind ...

'I was to ride a horse trained by David Nicholson, called Mac's Chariot, and I knew he was notoriously a tearaway. He had previously been trained in Ireland, and had been on the floor several times in races. But this was his first run of the season, and his first time ever in a race with me on board. When we talked before the race, David warned me to settle the horse but, partly due to the layout of the Wetherby course, that was easier said than done. He jumped the first well, and as there were no more than seven runners, I was happy to tuck him in last behind the bunch. But there is such a distance between the first and

33

second fences on this track that Mac's Chariot began to pull and tear impatiently.

'He was running so freely going to the second that I pulled him to the outside to allow more space. But he hardly lifted a leg as we hit the fence full on. Instead of being thrown forward and clear of the horse, as normally happens, I was still on board when he landed flat on his right side, trapping my right leg beneath him.

'Instantly, I knew that I would not ride again that day. Within 20 seconds or so, I knew the leg was broken. Fortunately, the horse had removed himself without twisting the leg any further, but as I bent to try and lift it by the knee, the foot didn't come. It sagged rather pitifully and told me the worst.

'When the ambulance men arrived, they were careful not to move the leg more than was essential. In fact, they tied my two legs together, then three men lifted me on to a stretcher. Back in the ambulance room, I had a jab, which quickly reduced the pain, and also had a cup of tea, which was a mistake. When I reached York Hospital, they told me I could not have an anaesthetic for three hours after taking any food—even tea. My operation was set for 6 p.m., but the admission of an emergency case delayed it still further and it was almost 7.30—about six hours after the fall—when I was finally wheeled into the theatre.

'As broken legs go, I suppose I was lucky. The fracture was low down, just above the ankle, and it was a clean break. I was home by Tuesday, but the worst was to come—20 weeks in plaster, and the sinking knowledge that I had ridden my last race for something like nine months.

'For the first month, I must have been difficult to live with. I checked the runners and riders every day, listened to the results every night and felt unfairly sour whenever a likely mount of mine came home for somebody else. But this maddening frustration steadily eased with the passing weeks, as I began to set myself recovery targets.

'It was the longest break from racing I had endured in 20 years, but I always believed I would ride again. When the heavy plaster came off, I was all for starting exercises, but the doctor insisted that I had a lightweight plaster on the ankle for another six weeks. It was an extra irritation at the time, but at this distance, I know he was right because there is scarcely a time when the ankle bothers me. A slight stiffness when I get out of bed is the only reminder of the fall, but any ache has normally disappeared by the time I reach the bathroom.

'Three weeks after that plaster came off, I got onto a horse again in the yard at home. It was a thoroughbred which I thought would give me a quiet ride, but the major problem was that I still could not bend the ankle.

'For several weeks, I went through a ritual in the bath, getting the water as hot as I could stand it to loosen the joints, then working my foot against the side. For a long time—or so it seemed—I just could not lift the toes, but gradually, the stiffness eased and movement returned.

'I suppose it was natural that I had a psychological barrier to overcome about falling off again. I had to find out whether the leg would stand it—but there is no way you can, or would want to, plan a heavy fall. Eventually, it happened quite naturally when a horse I was riding out near home slipped on greasy ground and, just like Mac's Chariot, fell on top of the leg. I can't say it didn't hurt, but I got up from it with no lasting ill effects and instantly felt more confident.

'My racing comeback was at Newton Abbot during the first week of the 1979–80 season, early in August, when the ground is hard and a fall is the last thing anyone wants. I was worried, I have to admit. It was impossible to put the leg out of my mind and pretend it had never happened. My fear was not so much the chance of another injury, but the possibility that I would not be able to do the job as well as before after those months off the track.

'That fear subsided after the first ride and never returned. I had a fall at Worcester in September, and another when I flew to Norway for a weekend meeting, but neither affected me badly and I soon felt as comfortable in the saddle as I had ever done.'

King accepts his awesome list of fractures without complaint or surprise. He broke his pelvis on the Grand National course at Liverpool, fractured his skull at Hereford—minor enough to allow him to ride a winner on his comeback, a month to the day later—and broke ribs at Sandown Park. In the first ten years of his career, he also broke his collarbone five times, and he touches wood wryly over his escape since then from the jockey's most common complaint.

'Often, the most frustrating injuries are not the breaks, but the strains and bruises. I have frequently torn the ligaments of my ankles and been kept out for three weeks—and even that is really too soon to go back to riding. On one occasion when I was riding as retained jockey to Bob Turnell, I reported fit for the following day's racing and Bob said he thought I was not ready to ride. I insisted that I should know my own recovery, and went ahead with the ride. For the first few minutes, it was one of the most painful experiences of my life. As the joints warmed up, the pain began to lessen, but I honestly thought I would never get round the course.

'That was not the only time that I rushed a recovery. One year, I was suffering from a bruised shin after being kicked by a horse as I fell. My first ride back was a good horse, but once on board, I found I could not bear my leg rubbing against the saddle—the pain was just too much. I completed the course with my leg sticking out sideways and must have looked absurdly clumsy ... but the horse still won.'

Nobody becomes a National Hunt jockey without expecting the

occasional fall. It is the occupational hazard most synonymous with the profession. But it is equally true that nobody relishes it—and that some are better at it than others.

'The idea that you can learn to fall and roll outside the confines of a race is a myth. You only learn when your own safety is at stake, and you only improve after the first few tumbles in races.

'If I know I am coming off, the thing paramount in my mind is that I hope to hell I am not hit from behind by another horse. As I land, I usually manage a sharp, almost instinctive glance back, and if there is a gap it is generally worth trying to throw myself out of the range of the horses still crossing the fence. If not, I curl into as tight a ball as possible, turning my back on the fence and tucking my head inside my arms. There are times when there is no escape, and you accept the inevitable foot in your back. Much more painful, and potentially dangerous, is the horse which kicks you as it passes over your body.

'I have seen riders, mainly young and inexperienced, fall off, then get straight up again in sheer panic, only to be knocked flat once more by another horse. I have also seen gruesome spectacles of jockeys who have had their faces kicked in while lying on the ground. It happened to Stan Mellor and it happened to Michael Scudamore—the latter so badly that he lost the full sight of one eye and had to retire from riding.

'Perhaps it is not surprising that so many stories circulate about jockeys losing their nerve, and maybe there are occasions when I would not blame somebody for simply feeling scared to get back in the saddle. Weighing-room gossip regularly links some unfortunate rider with such stories, but I have never personally known anyone who has given up through lack of nerve.

'I have, however, known a good deal of well-known jockeys who have quit because the aches and pains caused by the endless tumbles had grown unbearable. Riding had ceased being any kind of enjoyment ... and the day when that happens really is the day to get out.'

3 French follies?

Lingfield

To reach Lingfield Park from the western side of London, you pass under the package-tour-path out of Gatwick Airport, cross the Brighton Road and wind through a picturesque, old-fashioned English village.

The course itself, undulating and surrounded by trees, is among England's most beautiful and, on this December Saturday, had attracted a good number of top horses, despite the rival attraction of Cheltenham. My main interest, however, centred on a partnership which, without unkind exaggeration, had about as much hope of winning their race as I did. Cregg was the name of the horse, Mrs Sheilagh French the name of the jockey.

It was my first view of Mrs French, although she was anything but unknown to me. In the opinion of what seemed the majority of professional riders, she was 'a menace and a nuisance'.

A short, dark-haired lady, who appeared to be in her fifties, Mrs French and her daughter ride their own horses, chiefly in novice company and against the pros. 'They seldom finish a race,' one jockey told me, 'and I can only recall the family ever having a few winners, so I don't know how they afford it. But what is worse is that they cause endless problems to us by having so little skill or control over their horses.'

Mrs French, the elder, was at this time waiting to appear before the Jockey Club at Portman Square to explain a recent incident at Windsor where she allegedly pulled up her mount in front of a fence and took out at least one other rider at the same time. She stood, many believed, to lose her licence.

Unabashed, she marched into the parade ring at Lingfield, mounted Cregg a little awkwardly and was led—rather hastily it seemed to me—immediately out towards the course while the other jockeys were still circling their horses.

Cregg, it must be said, had little winning pedigree. He had, in fact, been pulled up three times in his previous five outings, and the remaining two were no more productive. Here, he was up against the redoubtable Beacon Light, an odds-on favourite, not to mention a good few others with immeasurably more impressive histories.

Mrs French, I learned, was none too popular with regular racegoers either. Eavesdropping on one heated discussion between a well-groomed couple, I overheard: 'It's her who should be stopped, not the poor horse. She's just a menace.' That word again.

As things transpired, Cregg and Mrs French had little chance to do much damage. The second fence accounted for them. Cregg hit it hard after swerving in to jump it, and Mrs French tumbled over in bone-shaking fashion and lay inert on the heavy, mud-caked turf for several seconds before rising somewhat shakily to her feet.

Beacon Light won with a good deal to spare, and everyone's thoughts had long since passed on from Mrs French and the hapless, hopeless Cregg. But I caught one further sight of her, emerging a little incongruously from the cluster around the winners' enclosure, mud flecking her face, and striding off in the direction of the stables to attend to her horse. Just for a moment, I felt sorry for her. Then, I reasoned, she wouldn't do it if the experience failed to give her some sort of kick ...

Sheilagh French, I discovered, was not the sort of woman to seek sympathy. When I ran her to ground at Folkestone two weeks later, she had just finished convincingly last in a three-mile 'chase. I entered the primitive, wooden dressing-room armed with platitudes, only to retreat a step or two as a finger jabbed me in the chest, animated eyes met mine and Mrs French announced that she had enjoyed 'a fabulous ride'.

Then, having insisted with suspicion that she could not help me, Sheilagh French proceeded to hold forth for a full half-hour on her life as a jockey, pausing only long enough to draw the occasional breath and allow me the odd word in a hundred.

Her age had to remain a secret, but she did tell me she began race-riding in 1949, which not only meant that she had completed 30 years as a jockey but also that she was riding when Jeff King—oldest of the regular male jockeys—was an eight-year-old in short trousers.

'We have to have an annual medical now before they renew our licence,' she revealed. 'Last year, I saw a doctor who told me I was punchdrunk from falling too much and that there was no way he would give me another licence the following year. When I got angry with him, he said I was hysterical, which was another sign of being punchdrunk. I wasn't going to have my life ruined by any damned doctor, so this year I took my daughter along and told her to sit and look pretty. I was passed fit without an argument.'

The daughter, Sarah—tall for a jockey, but slightly built and dark-haired like her mother—joined us at that moment complaining that she had just been sworn at by Jeff King over an incident during a race earlier that afternoon. King related later: 'I told her that she was welcome to kill herself on a course, but when other jockeys are involved it's different. I don't think she or her mother are strong or skilful enough to ride at this level.'

I asked Sheilagh if she was aware of being resented by a number of her male counterparts. She was. 'Most of the older riders are very nice—and so are the very young ones. It's the fellows who have found a little success and think they've made it who upset me. Do you know, I asked Steve Smith-Eccles to ride one of my horses a week or so ago and he wouldn't. Maybe it was beneath him ...'

There was apparently no racing tradition in the French family before Sheilagh—'and I didn't start very young' she confesses. But her career might have come to an abrupt end when she first rode in a point-to-point race.

'I used to get through a bottle of whisky a day without any trouble, and hadn't really considered the effect it might have on my riding. I was cold and nervous when I turned up for this point-to-point, so I went straight into the beer-tent and downed two double-scotches. It might not sound much, but I hadn't eaten for a day or so and it went straight to my head.

'When it came to mounting, I was given rather too vigorous a leg-up, and shot straight over the horse, landing the other side! I thought I had a chance in this race, but we had only cleared one fence when I tried to get my horse going, and instead of responding he stopped dead. I carried on and landed in a heap, complaining that I had been obstructed by another horse.

'It may sound funny now, but I learned my lesson. Ever since that day, I have never had a drink on the day of a race, or even on the night before. It's just the same as driving a car—it doesn't mix with alcohol on an empty stomach.'

I put it to Mrs French that she must have had her share of heavy falls over the years. Did she not sometimes think she might be better suited to a less harsh life?

'On a bad horse the life might be harsh,' she scoffed. 'But the idea is sheer nonsense when you have a decent ride. Today, I reached each fence grinning from ear to ear, just knowing he was going to fly over it. Now, that's the sort of feeling that makes it worthwhile. Mind you, I wasn't certain that this was going to be a good day. Down at the start, my horse was playing up badly—he's a lazy old thing you see—and for the first time in my life I had to whip a horse before a race. Then I swore at him loudly—I don't know what the other riders thought of me!'

With something approaching pride, Mrs French opened her mouth and showed me a front tooth that had been broken in half by a recent fall—albeit while hunting—and by merely watching and listening, I had to admit that her enthusiasm was infectious. With her hair tousled and unkempt, a blot of mud on her nose and an anorak over her civilian clothes, she continually prodded me with that forefinger to make her points.

She told me a good deal more as we stood in that murky changing-room on a December Tuesday. She was indignant over being called before a disciplinary committee over the fracas at Windsor; she was justly proud and precise in her recall of the occasions when she had beaten the top pros. It was a strange interview with an unusual woman. I went to see her with the notion that jump racing was not a feminine business, and came away with that opinion unaltered. Mrs French, that afternoon, did not look particularly feminine, but in her business I am sure she would not mind me saying so. She was, however, extremely stubborn and carried an unflagging belief in herself.

Sheilagh French also had news to dismay the men who undoubtedly wanted her out. 'On days like this one,' she told me, 'I feel I could go on riding until I'm 90.'

Dick Francis was at Lingfield on December 8, both to promote his new thriller and to preside over his own race—The Dick Francis Handicap Chase. Before the event, it diverted jockeys and punters alike to ponder the possibilities of the link.

Would the favourite be sabotaged? Would the jockeys be poisoned by the weighing-room tea? Or would sudden, blinding searchlights produce mass carnage at the water jump? Such unlikely proposals were prompted by the television serialisation of Francis's racing novels which was running at the time. Its exaggerated focus on the unethical sides of the game upset some jockeys, amused others. 'It makes it look as if every one of us is a crook,' complained one. But it was Richard Evans who suggested that the projection, despite its natural bias towards crime as an appeal to the audience, could do steeplechasing no harm at all. 'I am sure there are some people who believe that jump jockeys only ride in one race a year, and that is the Grand National,' he said. 'At least this series has focused some attention on the sport.'

In the event, a 14-year-old horse won the Francis Chase, which was stunning enough, and a certain suspense was created by a steward's inquiry, though for nothing more sinister than an allegation that the winner had 'taken the ground' of the second horse. Steven Smith-Eccles, the jockey of the runner-up, and a target for Mrs French's tongue, must have wished he had not bothered to object—the stewards fined him £20 for 'being frivolous'. It was, however, an instance of the competitive spirit that had inspired the young and boisterous Smith-Eccles into second place in the jockeys' championship. We were to hear a great deal more from him before the season expired.

The Young Pretender—Smith-Eccles

For most of us, a mild shock or a disappointment of some nature can lead to a period of taking stock of life's values. For Smith-Eccles, the prompt came from a broken neck. It happened in the spring of 1979 at an unimportant meeting in Devon, and it suddenly made him realise just what a dangerous mission he had taken on when he became a jump jockey.

Smith-Eccles, knows as 'SS' in the weighing-room, is the most unlikely owner of a double-barrelled name I've ever met. Short and stocky, boyish and boisterous, he is the son of a Derbyshire miner and his factory-worker wife, and shatters preconceived illusions of a horsey family with the remark: 'The only racing in our house was the ten bob my dad would have on for the telly races each Saturday afternoon.'

When Steve broke his neck, his season ended more than two months early. 'It gave me a lot of time to think. I knew I had got off lightly—the break was not a severe one. But if it had gone differently, I could have been in a wheelchair for the rest of my life. It never made me even consider giving up, but I think it changed my priorities a bit. Now, although I am as ambitious as anyone, my great aim is to stay in one piece while I'm in this job. It's no good arriving at 28 years old with a battered body and a fuddled brain.'

We were talking seven days before Christmas. 'SS', with 43 winners, was just five behind the current leader in the Jockeys' Championship, Jonjo O'Neill. At 24, he was the new, young pretender to the throne—a surprise even to the bookies, who had offered ante-post odds of 50 to 1 against him being champion.

Thankfully, it had not changed him one bit. He is lively, cheerful, with a likeable hint of cockiness set off by a generally earthy attitude to life. 'Of course, I want to be champion. But there is so far to go, it's not worth worrying about at this stage. If I'm still up there come March, then I'll have a dart at it.'

It was the Saturday television sessions which fashioned the destiny of Steve. 'I used to watch with dad, and I remember saying to him that I would be a jockey one day. It might have been one of the few things open to me. I was so small I was always laughed at while I was at school. I loved football, and used to be quite good on the right wing. But when I got as far as a trial for Derbyshire Schools, they told me I was too small for that, as well.'

'When I was 15, I joined a yard at Newmarket as a stable-lad. It was one of the few mixed yards around, with both flat horses and jumpers, but I knew I was going to be too heavy to make a career of the flat.

'I had one flat ride—the first and last of my career. It was at Yarmouth, and I had to lose eight pounds in four days to make the weight. I managed it by running, sweating and not eating a thing ... but it didn't help the horse.'

Steeplechasing, with its less severe weight demands, suits Smith-

Eccles a good deal better. 'I eat and drink like a pig,' he admits. 'I don't have to worry about my weight now—I'm pretty constant around ten stone and that's good enough.'

After his first winner, on a horse called Ballysilly at Market Rasen when he was 19, his progress was steady until the breakthrough came at the start of the 1979–80 season. 'I got a good retainer with Nicky Henderson, who trains a lot of decent horses. I was bound to start riding a few more winners, and when that happens, you're suddenly popular. Everyone wants a fashionable jockey.'

His face broke into a grin when I referred to the distinctive, vigorous riding style which seemed to suit his personality. 'That's what they all say,' he replied. 'It developed quite naturally, I never really thought about it. All I know is that if I'm in there with a chance, I give it all I've got.'

Smith-Eccles lives in Newmarket, centre for the flat but an outpost of National Hunt racing. It is the bane of his life. 'Apart from Fakenham and Huntingdon, there isn't a course within $1\frac{1}{2}$ hours of my house,' he says.

'I am one of very few jump jockeys in that area, which means I have to drive everywhere alone. I might be up at five some days, and not back until nine or ten at night. During a season, I get through 50–60,000 miles, and it is easily the worst part of the job. It makes me bored and very tired—much more tired than the actual racing. I have a Datsun and I drive it like stink. It goes like hell and it has to—maybe I drive the same way as I ride.'

I asked him what his interests were outside racing, and the brief answer was that he didn't have time for any. 'During the season, the week normally involves six days of travelling and riding, and Sunday, when the phone never stops ringing. We have seven weeks off each year, and I like to get abroad in the sun for three of those, before getting back to cock my leg over a horse again.'

Steve is unmarried, but lives with his girlfriend, Di, and insists: 'In this job, you need a good woman to look after you. If she didn't cook and wash and clean, I would never get any of it done. By the end of a day's riding and driving, I'm in no state for any of that.'

Did Di worry about his job and its inherent risk? He frowned, and thought for a moment before answering: 'Outwardly, no she doesn't. But although she never says anything to me about it, I think she does fret a bit when I have a fall—I don't think there is a jockey's wife who doesn't.

'I thrive on the excitement of this game. I could never do anything else. But I have to admit it's a bloody dangerous way to earn a living.'

Much maligned, but indomitably enthusiastic, Mrs Sheilagh French (right) and her daughter Sarah, in the family racing colours.

Animated and talkative as ever, Steve Smith-Eccles makes a point after winning the Sun Alliance Chase on Sweet Joe at the 1978 Cheltenham.

4 Breaking point

Jeff King was reading *The Sporting Life* while a friend drove him to Nottingham on December 10. It was a day of no great promise. Just one ride, and that on a nervy and uninspired novice hurdler, filled him with little optimism of coming home with anything more than his riding fee. But, as he glanced down the day's card in the newspaper, something disturbing caught his eye.

Flitgrove, an experienced, staying horse, was declared to run in the afternoon's feature event. The rider's name next to him was Peter Scudamore, recently turned professional and enjoying a prolific start to the season. The sight of the name did not please King, although he had nothing personal against Scudamore. It meant, quite simply, that King had been 'jocked off'.

King had ridden Flitgrove in all of his five previous races this season. The results had not been startingly good—two third places, three times unplaced—but that did not appease him. No jockey likes to lose a ride on a familiar horse, particularly one with big-race plans. King was also troubled by discovering his fate through reading *The Sporting Life*.

'There are obviously some horses which you ride once for a particular reason, perhaps because the stable jockey is injured, and you do not really expect to ride him again. But Flitgrove is a mount I have grown to expect. He ran in the National last year, while I sat at home with my broken leg still not mended. I remember urging him on with one half of my mind, while the other felt sore that I was not riding him myself.

'It makes it doubly annoying to lose the ride when, as happened here, he is declared for a low-class race.'

With Scudamore claiming the four-pound allowance due to any jockey who has not ridden 20 winners, Flitgrove won at 10 to 1. King watched the race from the stand and decided against confronting trainer David Nicholson on the spot but chose his moment later.

Things were not going well for King. As we drove to Worcester two days later, it had been 16 rides and ten racing days since his last winner. His services were certainly not being ignored or passed over, but few of the rides he was being offered could seriously be considered for the winners' enclosure.

'But,' as he said, 'this game can have you fooled. Many times, I've gone through a long spell like this, without a winner, and then in a matter of a couple of hours, you win two races and everything has changed.'

A few hours later, King had ridden one winner and one third, and was due to ride a warm favourite at Uttoxeter the following day. If it could not accurately be said that everything had changed, a distinct improvement had, at least, occurred.

Not that it hadn't been a curious day. King's winner was Pencraig, a horse whose stable jockey, Graham Thorner, had declined to ride because he did not care for him. Starting as second favourite, he stayed on well in heavy ground to win by four lengths. The owner, Lord Belper, was delighted, yet showed it in an odd way. As King dismounted with a comment on how well the horse had jumped, Lord Belper responded: 'He must have jumped well to win with you on him!' 'I think he was taking the mickey,' said King later, 'but I had to look at him again to be sure!'

In the day's last race, King was having a difficult time on a three-year-old called Darby Green, a poignant ride as his trainer, Vernon Cross, was unconscious in a Sussex hospital having suffered a stroke a week earlier. A reluctant racehorse, Darby Green insisted on dropping his head between his knees spasmodically for the first of the two miles, but King finally righted him and moved through from last place to challenge the leaders. At the final hurdle, he had some chance, but two better finishers pulled clear, leaving Darby Green an obvious third.

As is customary when finishing comfortably, King sat up and relaxed the pressure with the aim of allowing the horse to canter past the post. Darby Green had other ideas. He stopped in his tracks. It was a moment of inspired absurdity, with King obliged to produce his whip again and force his mount over the line, eventually only a few lengths clear of the fourth horse who had long since given up hope of a place.

It was that evening, after racing had finished, that King realised all was not well with Graham Thorner. Champion jockey in 1971 and rider of the Grand National winner a year later, Thorner had seen plenty of good times in his long career with trainer Tim Forster. Now, he told King, he felt tired and unwell and thought he should rest for a week. Three days later, after riding at Nottingham, he announced his retirement.

Forster was quoted as saying: 'We could not look at each other as we stood in the paddock together for the last time. He'd been with me for 14 years and nobody could have given more than Graham did.'

King explained: 'I was surprised by the news, but in another way I understood. Graham had always had a hell of a lot of rides, and had never been content to have an easy run round. He rode them all with a furious determination—he used to give them a lot of stick until he quietened down in recent years—and he was never satisfied to be anything but best.'

'Maybe all the travelling got him down eventually—I don't think it was the falls. He was a hard man and certainly wasn't frightened of getting hurt. But he did break his leg twice, and I know for a fact that it was giving him a lot of pain at the end.

'His real trouble was that he didn't enjoy the job any more. Graham, you see, was never much of a socialiser, and to me, that is a very important part of the life. If you can't enjoy a laugh and a drink after racing, or on the way home, then your mind stays set on the horses you have ridden, the mistakes you may have made, tomorrow's rides and all your other problems. It's no surprise when it all gets on top of you if you don't relax, and Graham was the type who devoured work. If he wasn't riding, he'd be toiling away on his farm at home ... he never stopped, and I can't think it was good for him.

'But he had been to the top, done everything and seen everything in racing. Getting out now may be the best thing he could do.'

Within a week, Thorner announced that he was feeling better, although he certainly had no intention of going back on his decision. But, while one jump jockey was content to have quit the game, another was waiting with fretful impatience to get back.

Jim Fox

I arrived in the Hampshire village of Fyfield as dusk was settling on an icy January day. There is precious little to see in Fyfield—one pub and a few houses in fact—but it does have one claim to fame. The stables of Toby Balding, one of steeplechasing's most successful trainers, are based there. So too, is Jimmy Fox.

Fox was a jump jockey for more than a decade until, at the age of 32, the Jockey Club doctor decided that he was unfit to continue riding and refused to renew his licence. Despite the security of a job as assistant trainer to Balding, Fox was shattered. He had never challenged the household names of the sport, but was fiercely proud of his successes, which included the considerable feat of winning the Mackeson and Hennessy Gold Cups on the same horse, Red Candle, in the early seventies. A painting of Fox on Red Candle hangs above the fireplace in the house where Jimmy, his wife Trish and two children live, in the grounds of the stables.

When I phoned to arrange a meeting with Fox, his wife told me he was under sedation, having dislocated his shoulder at work with a horse. It was, she said, not the first time it had happened. She could not be sure, but this must be either the seventh or eighth such injury.

She assured me that her husband would talk to me the following after-noon, but when I kept the appointment, it seemed for some while that I had made a wasted journey. Fox was quite obviously reluctant to talk.

After a considerable wait, I was invited by Toby Balding to join Fox and himself on their evening rounds of the 70 horses currently resident. It was a fascinating tour, Balding solemnly introducing me to each horse and providing a thumb-nail sketch of family histories and racing careers. Fox, his arm in a sling and a hat pulled low over his eyes, spoke little.

I watched as he performed the difficult task of shovelling out the horses' feed with one hand, an individual diet for each animal, then retired to the warmth of the house and set about breaking the ice.

Fox, who was clearly struggling to overcome a basic mistrust of journalists, was born in Waterford, Southern Ireland and, like a number of other jockeys, dabbled successfully in showjumping before turning to racing. His employer of the time, a man named Dennis Quigley, apparently discouraged Fox from riding in point-to-points 'because he always feared he would lose me to racing'.

As Fox unwound and began to speak more freely, the impact that enforced retirement had made on his life became obvious. He was bitter about the decision and, something that was to surprise a number of other jockeys, determined to prove that he should have his licence back.

He was, in fact, prepared to enter hospital for an operation through which the joints of his troublesome shoulder would be bound together forever. 'It might mean,' he agreed, 'that I will never be able to lift my arm enough to scratch my back, but I will have all the movement necessary to ride. Then if they still say I can't have a licence, I shall want to know why.'

I asked about Fox's other injuries and he steadily related the list. A fractured skull, partial blindness in the right eye, various minor breaks and bruises ... and concussion on upwards of 25 separate occasions. 'They asked me at the medical how many times I had been concussed and I couldn't tell them, because it is often difficult to know. Even if you are sure, you frequently say nothing for fear of losing rides. Unless it was bad, I generally used to carry on.'

'The only time it was really rough was when I came off a horse I was schooling. I woke up in the washrooms of the stables and didn't have a clue how I'd got there. I looked at myself in the mirror and I was bleeding from the ears. I couldn't remember what I had been doing or where I was going, so I went to ask some of the lads. They thought I was joking, but it was several days later that I woke up with my memory restored.

'I know the doctors at the medical were trying to make out that I was punchdrunk. But if I'm not fit to ride, how is it that I can school young, wild horses over fences at home—that is equally as demanding as race-riding. I can understand how some jockeys get burned out—Graham Thorner quitting didn't surprise me at all, because he had been racing up and down the country non-stop, taking rides anywhere and everywhere. I have never done that, and I never would. I want to ride again for my pleasure.

'I've had the usual injuries that we all accept in this job. And the eye trouble was caused by a stone kicked up by a horse when I was riding at Kempton. If you threw a ball to me, I probably wouldn't be able to catch it, but I still maintain I am capable of judging distances, which is the important thing in this game.'

Fox, who rode his last winner in 1977, admits that there is one thing in the job which he disliked intensely. 'The travelling sometimes seems endless,' he says, 'and I'm no lover of driving.' But he was patently prepared to put up with that.

'Compared to some jockeys, I've been lucky with injuries. I have seen blokes with half their head kicked away. Michael Scudamore was completely unrecognisable after the fall and kicking which finished his career. But the thought of that doesn't deter me. The falls are something that you learn to live with; after a while, you don't think about them at all.

'There are some amusing sides to it, too. I was once riding at Leicester, and David Mould was having a dreadful afternoon. It think his first three mounts had fallen, and he was sitting glumly in a corner of the changing room when another rider, whose neck was broken and plastered, wandered in for a chat. David got up and chased him out, yelling that he would only bring him more bad luck. It didn't do him any good, because I recall his last two fell, too.

'Some jockeys are very superstitious, but it generally didn't affect me too much. I only had one rule, which was that if I realised I had forgotten something on my way to racing, I would never turn back, no matter how important it might be. But I must confess that when Trish pointed out a magpie in our path on the road to Newbury one day, I swore it was a black and white crow!'

I went away from Fyfield into the frosty night, having warmed to Fox and his obsessional desire to get back in the saddle. But privately, I still believed that he was mad to try.

Graham Thorner

Graham Thorner's retirement, and the reasons behind it, formed the most chilling comment of the winter on the jump jockey profession. He was only 30 years old and there was little to suggest he was not still at his peak ... until, that is, you studied the man closely. His face looked painfully thin, stark and haunted and his body had wasted alarmingly. Thorner got out before the job left him permanently damaged.

I gave him two months and then asked him to reflect on his career, and the pressures which led him to quit. The first striking impression was that he knew he had done the right thing, at the right time.

'I'm feeling a lot healthier now—just about 100 per cent better,' he

49

explained in an accent fruitily betraying his Somerset background, where his family farmed near Cheddar. 'But I have no regrets about anything I have done. I don't make decisions without giving them a lot of thought, you see. Anything I do has to be right.'

That was my emphatic introduction to a man who, in the words of television commentator and *Sunday Times* writer Brough Scott, lives his life 'like a car with the choke full out'.

Thorner, too, draws a motoring analogy to illustrate the problems he encountered. 'Alright, I was only 30 when I quit—but years are not relevant. One person may keep a car in perfect condition for ten years, just driving it down to the shops and back twice a week. Another will drive his car into the ground and clap out the engine within three years.'

'It was that way with me. I was champion at the age of 21 and I was going flat out. I can't just tick over in my work, having a break here and there and maybe not trying so much on certain horses. It isn't in me to be that way.

'I never like to be sat still. But I also wouldn't walk across the room unless there was a reason for doing so—and I'd want to do two jobs on the way. If I can get two days' work into one, then I will—and I would make sure the work was good. I'm sure I'd be like it in anything I chose to do. If I started to sell sweets, I would work hard enough to make damn sure I sold more than the guy next door. I like to think that is why I was a successful jockey.'

Successful, he certainly was. At the age of 15 he left school and 'decided to find out what this racing game was all about'. He rode as an amateur for just one season, and had only three winners in 80 starts. 'Everyone advised me to stay as an amateur, not to commit myself to the life. But I needed to know if racing wanted me, and I had to give it everything.' So Thorner turned pro and began his lasting partnership with bachelor Tim Forster, the Wantage trainer. In all, Thorner rode 650 winners, the most famous among them being Well To Do in the 1972 Grand National.

'To Mrs Bloggs down the road, or even the fellow who has a punt at the bookies, that must be the highlight of my career—because it is the only time I have crept onto their televisions on the news programme, not just under a jockey's cap on Saturday afternoon. They remember me for that—but I prefer to think of the previous season, when I was champion.

'That was an opinion of me stretched over nine months of effort, nine months of good and bad horses. The National, despite all the atmosphere, all the trimmings and all the headlines, is just one more race when you boil it down.'

Thorner was never plagued by weight worries, nor was he troubled by falls. 'I broke most of the bones in my body but I never dreaded coming off. I believe it is a tough business and I didn't mind that side of it at all. Life is too soft. Thank God there is still something like that for the tough ones.'

What he did dislike was the interminable travelling. Despite living near Jeff King in Wiltshire, a fairly central launching pad for most of England's race courses, Thorner exceeded 50,000 miles in most steeplechasing seasons—and grew to heartily hate driving.

'Now that I've given up, you will very rarely find me driving at all. It made me so bored and so tired that I will now do anything to get out of the driver's seat. If my wife is with me, she will always drive—even if it's just down to the shops and back.'

'But the worst thing about the job was the periods of depression when I couldn't ride a winner and everyone was on my back. I was the one stable jockey for Tim Forster's yard, so when I was available I rode them all. If the stable was out of form, and the horses were not going well, then I would have a bad run—it was as simple as that.

'In racing, the jockey tends to get the blame for failures because he is the obvious and easiest target. It doesn't matter if there are a dozen other reasons why the horse hasn't gone well, more often than not it is the jockey who is made scapegoat. But the truth of it is that anyone can pick a fault in the riding of any jockey in any race. I know, I have stood and criticised the best, just to prove the point.'

When it came to the time to quit, Thorner did not waste a day. 'I was riding on the Monday, thinking I might go on for another two or three years. By Tuesday, I had decided to pack up.'

'Tim Forster and I had a very sensible discussion and decided it was the right way out. I felt so ill that I could not enjoy life, let alone riding. I had a stomach ulcer which meant that eating did me no good at all. When I weighed in for the last time, I was 8st. 9lb. stripped—about a stone under my normal minimum weight.

'Although I had made up my mind, I didn't want anyone to know. I talked to Jeff King on the Wednesday at Worcester and one half of me wanted to discuss it with him. But I didn't, I just compromised by telling him I needed a few days' rest.

'People say it was a brave decision and I suppose it was. Lots of the boys have said to me since that this is the way they would like to do things. But you can bet very few of them will.

'Of course, it has caused me problems. I had plans to look for another farm before I finished riding, then to make gallops and combine farming with training. But there was no time. I haven't sorted out my future yet, but I would like to try buying and selling horses.

'Whatever happens, I shan't cut myself off from racing. I'm not the sort who will turn his back on his past life just because times have changed. I had a lot of good years in racing and I'm thankful. But I couldn't go on in the state I was in.'

5 Shades of success

Lorna Vincent
Unmistakeably the girl in a hurry, Lorna Vincent passed us on the outskirts of Chepstow, her Ford Capri whipping down the centre of the road and threatening to enrage the patiently queuing racegoers until they saw the distinctive number plate—LJV 2—not to mention the silver horse and jockey mounted on the bonnet.

In her fashionable velvet jacket and dark skirt, her flushed young face pretty and eager, she did not look the sort who was about to get on a horse and put her life on the line yet again. A career girl, maybe, but a steeplechase jockey? Never.

It had, in fact, been something of an accident. A jockey, Lorna will insist, was the last thing she wanted to be when she began work as a stable-girl for Les Kennard in Somerset, early in 1976. And being the only regular girl professional, with 14 winners from the early stages of the season and a string of trainers waiting to offer her rides, was not even a wild dream.

Her aim, quite simply, had been to make enough money to buy a horse for her first love of the time … show jumping. It was in this sport that she hoped to make a career and she only arrived at Kennard's stables when tragedy struck with the death of her beloved horse, Samantha. 'I didn't even like racing at the time—I used to think it all a bit futile.'

Her attitudes changed rapidly as her involvement with Kennard's small but successful band of racehorses grew. Yet still, she never considered race-riding herself.

'It was a complete shock to me when the guv'nor asked me to ride on the flat. I had never asked for a ride—never even wanted one, really. And, to tell you the truth, it very nearly put me off for good. I hated that flat race. We came out of the gate and that was it. Finished. I could see no excitement or interest in that at all. I only had two rides on the flat and that was too many, so I was hardly delirious when I rode my first over jumps. But it changed everything. The horse's name was Pretty Cute, and he won for me on August 17, 1978. I shall never need reminding of that date.'

A substantial amount had happened to Lorna Vincent in the interim, and she was acutely aware and apprehensive that people might say it had swollen her head. That, it had not. She was still a cheery, fun-loving west country girl—although born in Reading—who, at the jockeys' Christmas ball, cheekily raised her evening dress to her senior colleagues ... and revealed a pair of red longjohns underneath.

On December 15, she had ridden Walnut Wonder to victory in the rich SGB Hurdle at Ascot, to the astonishment of all but herself and her trainer. Wonder started at 33 to 1 and was not given a chance by the experts but, after the elimination of three favourites by falls, Lorna comfortably held off the fancied Lumen, to the embarrassment of his distinguished owner-trainer team of Peter Hopkins and Josh Gifford.

Inevitably, there were claims that the result would have been very different but for the falls, that Walnut Wonder's victory had been won almost bloodlessly. The snipes needled Lorna more than she would say, and at Chepstow she took the chance to prove a point as the horse won another competitive hurdle.

'I hated people saying that we were lucky—for the horse's sake as much as for mine. I know how good that horse is, and I wanted to show everyone else,' she told me as another bottle of champagne was delivered.

She mixed some champagne with her dubonnet, and giggled. 'I can drink more than most jockeys because I don't have many weight problems,' she said. 'I enjoy a drink, too—I also like eating sweets and crisps, all the things that jockeys should avoid. But I am a vegetarian.'

I asked her whether it had taken time for the men, many of them hardened, soured pros, to accept her as part of the scene in their domain. She thought briefly before replying that, almost without exception, they had been friendly and helpful. 'There were times early on when I sensed I was not accepted, but I have only once been torn apart by another rider after a race ... and that was Jeff King.'

'It happened after my third ride over fences, which I won. At one point in the race, I had moved across to the inside, believing that Jeff's mount was too far behind for me to interfere with him. But straight after the finish, Jeff tackled me, and swore at me for being stupid and dangerous and not riding in a straight line. It completely took away the pleasure of winning, and I felt really upset. I knew I was in the wrong, and I plucked up courage to approach Jeff in the bar and apologise. He just laughed and told me not to take anything to heart, because he had only said it for my own good. Since then, we've got on tremendously well.

'I worry a great deal about what people think of me. I hate the thought that someone might dislike or resent me. I haven't changed, you see. I don't feel any different for having won a few races. I'm still just a stable girl, and I have no desire to be anything else.

'Sometimes at home around the stables, I will do anything to avoid talking about a winner of mine, because I fear the other lads and girls will think badly of me. They are mostly genuinely pleased whenever I win, but I don't want anyone to turn against me. Race-riding, after all, still takes up only a small part of my life. The rest is the hard slog of looking after horses—and I still get just as much of a kick out of one of my horses winning for someone else as from having a winning ride myself.'

Injuries had, up to then, occurred as relatively minor irritations, if three separate back injuries and a trampled leg can be so casually dismissed, but it still surprised me that Lorna so easily and obviously rejected the fear element. 'I used to think it would worry me a lot, but after the second or third fall, I found I simply didn't think about it any more. I think that is the only way to get by.

'I've only once been really frightened. I started well in a race at Newton Abbot, where the course is tight and narrow and there was a field of 23 horses. I was in front when I came off at the second hurdle, and there was no way out. I just lay there, curled up, feeling them all come over the top of me. I would never like to go through that again.

'There are two things I could never do—that's ride in the Grand National, or really flog a tired horse with the whip. There are times when I know I ought to use the whip more than I do. But I'm not very good at bringing it through, and quite apart from that, I feel too much for the horses to give them a whang.

'The National frightens me, just to watch it on television. I shut my eyes when they get to each fence. Once, it was only the horses I worried about, but now that I know the other side of the story, I'm scared for the riders too. I have great admiration for every one who rides in that race—I think it is one of the bravest things any sportsman can do. I know that if I went out on the course, I would get to the start and freeze. I would just think "I can't do it." My father always says that the word "can't" doesn't exist—but in this case, it does for me.'

John Francome
The first time I met John Francome, he drove me to Taunton in a car with automatic windows, quadrophonic speakers and frightening speeds. He chatted easily in his ripe west country accent, hurrying back from Somerset because he had to lecture the boys at Eton School.

The next time I saw him, he was dressed in outrageous drag. It was the jockeys' Christmas Ball and Francome flounced on stage, with rouge, red lipstick and rotating bottom, to complete a mock strip at one in the morning. Two days later, I saw him again, being brought down in the Welsh Grand National at Chepstow and rushed to hospital with a dislocated shoulder that was to leave him inactive for almost a month. Inactive, that is, in racing terms only, as I found out when I drove to Lambourn, the racing village in the heart of the Berkshire countryside

The first professional girl jump jockey, Lorna Vincent.

John Francome, King's choice as Britain's most complete jockey, and Ballyfin Lake – both at full stretch.

and home for England's steeplechase champion jockey.

Francome's home, for seven years, had been a red, corrugated iron bungalow at the top of the sort of track which kids you it is leading nowhere. The bungalow, however, was never intended as a permanent arrangement and Francome was aiming to move, in February 1980, a distance of something like 50 yards to another world. He had built, virtually with his own hands, an impressive house of Cotswold stone, four-bedroomed and spacious and designed, by Francome, to blend with his other recent creations and constructions, an indoor riding school and 20 stable boxes with graceful archways and courtyards.

It had taken him seven summers of hard labour, together with every other spare hour he could squeeze from the hectic life of a jockey. It had cost him a good deal of money but, as we surveyed his work, he told me with justifiable pride: 'I don't owe anyone a penny. Everything is paid for from the money I have made out of racing.' It was a remarkable testimony to the success of a man who had reached the age of 27 only a month earlier.

The son of a builder, Francome's only family link with horses concerns his grandfather, who operated a haulage business with horse and cart. Yet, after a precocious entry into gymkhanas, he was showjumping in accomplished fashion by the age of 13 and might have followed that sport as a career but for the realism which has coloured all of his life.

'I knew that to be successful in showjumping I needed a lot of money, and that would have meant relying on my parents to an extent that I didn't want. So when I was 15, I left school and started work as a stable-lad with Fred Winter. I've been riding for him ever since.'

Francome's first ride, in late 1970, was on a horse called Multigray. 'It was trained just a few miles from my parents' house, and I had often ridden out on him. When we won, the owner gave me three sacks of potatoes!' The introduction to steeplechasing was not entirely straightforward, however. 'When I came into the sport, I had never heard of Fred Winter. I'd never even had enough interest in racing to watch it on television. The riding style and position is vastly different to that used in showjumping, and it took me a long time to adjust.'

The man who did most to shape Francome's career was Richard Pitman, his predecessor as stable jockey to Winter, and now a racing presenter on BBC television. John says: 'Richard gave me a lot of good advice, not just about riding itself, but about general behaviour and politeness. He taught me to chat people up, which can be the most important part of this job.'

'You have to get on with trainers if you are to ride their horses, and I've always been on good terms with most of them. Then, of course, you have to chat to the owners in the paddock before each race, and if you don't have anything to say the whole thing is very embarrassing.

The owners are always nervous for their horse, and I try to say something to make them laugh, without being cheeky or disrespectful. Richard was once asked by an owner what he thought the chances of a winner were, and he replied: "I am good enough sir, if your horse is!" '

Unlike many jumping jockeys, Francome never rode on the flat. 'The last time I was light enough to get a flat ride was when I was seven years old,' he says, with only a hint of humour. 'I have always had a problem with my weight, and if there is one thing I dislike about this job, it is having to go without my food. I don't deprive myself of anything in particular, but I always have to be careful when, and how much, I eat. It sometimes gets me down that I can't even have a cup of tea when I feel like one.

'My lowest riding weight even now is 10st. 8lb., which makes it a little surprising that I had more rides than anyone last season. But when I started out, I was 11st. stripped, and I had to go on a crash diet. It made me feel bad, physically ill, and I didn't fully recover for several years.

'Whatever I eat has to be in small quantities. As I always miss out lunch when I'm riding, I need something for breakfast, and I find that eating grapefruit, followed by one egg and one slice of bacon, is better for my weight than confining myself to toast and coffee.

'A lot of riders use sauna baths to sweat off some weight, but I avoid them like the plague. They give me headaches and make me feel worse than when I went in.

'I'm not averse to all the travelling, which I know sickens some jockeys. I quite like driving, and I would certainly rather drive than sit as a passenger. But my other main dislike is the cold weather that we so often have to put up with. It's not so bad at racing, where you will inevitably get warm during your first ride, but when I am riding out on the roads on a frosty morning, I sometimes think I must be mad.'

Francome is married to an attractive dark-haired girl called Miriam, once a secretary in Lambourn but now a model, but he confesses to being something of a social recluse. 'I don't go out a great deal at nights, chiefly because I'd always be worrying about my weight if we went to eat. I'm also virtually teetotal. The very occasional glass of lager and lime is all I'll have, and my reason is very simple—I just don't like the taste of alcohol.'

As he sat at his kitchen table sipping tea in anorak, sweater and jeans, John looked totally relaxed. The impression was confirmed as we talked about nerves. 'That is something I have never suffered from, before any race—not even the Grand National. Just as Richard Pitman did before me, I take the view that what will be, will be—and there is nothing I can do to change it, so why worry?'

'A lot of the time, jockeys' nerves can be traced back to the people they ride for. My guv'nor, Mr Winter, must be the best in the world. He understands racing totally, is completely fair and very loyal— I reckon we've only had two fall-outs in ten years. But if an owner has a big bet on a horse which gets beaten, there are plenty of trainers who will make the jockey their scapegoat and blame him for the defeat.

'Let's face it, if you have tried your best and finished fourth, and know you are going to get a bollocking for it, it's pretty demoralising and enough to make you feel nervous next time you ride. Funnily enough, it's a vicious circle, because the lower you are down the riding scale, the less chance you have of convincing the owner that it was not your fault his horse didn't win. In these circumstances, the struggling jockey has everything against him.'

Francome, who had been champion twice and runner-up three times in the past five years, feels no pressure from his success. 'On the contrary, it helps in all walks of life. If I go to a shop or a tradesman wanting some service, I'm far more likely to get things done quickly if I'm recognised.'

It had, however, had one detrimental effect. 'I realise now that I had begun to take things for granted,' he confessed. 'I don't think I was riding poorly, but I had lost some of the urge to win. The cure came in an unlikely way, from my two injuries this season. I missed a month with back trouble, then just as I was riding well again and chasing Jonjo O'Neill in the Championship, I did my shoulder. It was the most painful fall of my career. For the two hours before they put the bone back, I was in such agony that I wanted to pass out. I've had a good bit of time to think since then, and I believe it has given me a kick up the backside. I'm studying the formbook again, taking notice of all the horses that are running, and really looking forward to getting fit and riding again. We all need incentives, and I think I had run a bit short.'

Francome kids nobody about his future, which will not entirely lie in horseracing. 'Some jockeys eat and sleep the sport, and go on riding to an age when they are not fit to do anything else, either mentally or physically. I don't intend to let that happen to me. I'm an optimist about racing, but a realist too. You don't get long at the top in any sport, and my aim is simply to be completely successful while I'm there. I enjoy making money.

'I have one real ambition left. Obviously, I'd like to be champion again, and I'd like to win the National. But I'm not consumed by either of those aims. All I ever wanted out of racing was to ride six winners in one afternoon. So far, I've never managed more than three, but who knows, it might happen one day.'

With his riding school and his stables, let alone the property value, Francome would not starve if he retired tomorrow. But he has new ambitions driving him on now. 'Soon,' he says, 'I want to find a business interest outside racing completely. I'm not obsessed by the game, you see.'

Jonjo O'Neill

Southwell is steeplechasing at its most rustic. Turn north-east from Nottingham, I was told, drive ten miles on that road then follow the race signs. Those signs, I was to discover, led the unwitting driver through the kind of hedged-in maze to put Hampton Court to shame. Through four hamlets, past countless cattle and finally round a tight bend to a level crossing, where an antique board announces your destination.

The image is confirmed inside. The course buildings are really no more than a row of one-level wooden shacks, the 'grandstand' merely a bank of steps with a rickety roof. Primitive it may be, but it also gave me the feeling that this, rather than the space-age facilities of Sandown and Ascot, is what National Hunt is really about.

If the jockeys were slow to agree, I could not blame them. Their quarters were simply another shed, partitioned into one area for changing, another for weighing, and all of it on the sort of stone floor that, I suspect, might account for chilblains if not fallen arches.

I found Jonjo O'Neill there, in earnest discussion with one of the many trainers scrambling to employ him. He is small, as one would expect, and impeccably neat, his short, curled hair framing a round Irish face and a permanent mischievous grin. In every sense, the grin was justified. O'Neill was so comfortably clear at the head of the Championship that the bookies had ensured he was no longer worth a wager. He had managed to avoid injury while his most pressing opponents, Steve Smith-Eccles and John Francome, had both been sidelined, and he had just claimed a significant payout from State Express, one of the sport's newer sponsors, by riding his 55th winner of the season several furlongs ahead of anyone else. Life, on that misty January afternoon, looked good for Jonjo.

The most striking thing about the man is his obsession with the job. Quite unlike current champion John Francome, O'Neill would have been content just to make a simple living as a jockey. He even goes so far as to say: 'I would do the job for nothing if I had to.'

Jonjo, called plain Jon by many of his colleagues, was born in Fermoy, County Cork, in April of 1952. His interest in racing was almost certainly fostered by his father, for his three brothers 'would not know one end of a horse from the other'.

Jockey life began at the age of 15. Four years on the flat, around the Irish circuit, bore poor fruit. 'I had about one ride a month,' he recalls. 'No more than 70 in all.' It was, however, perhaps an omen that his first Irish ride over jumps was a winner.

At 19, it occurred to O'Neill that it might be an idea to seek a trade. 'I had never been an academic at school and had few qualifications. I began to think that I was getting nowhere and, although I had never wanted to be anything but a jockey, I had almost resigned myself to giving it up.'

Gordon Richards, not to be confused with the famous Sir Gordon, gave O'Neill his break. Nothing much, at first—a job as a lad in fact, at his stables in Penrith. Jonjo's few rides included only one winner, and that was taken away on an objection, and at the end of his first season, he prepared to head back to Ireland, with no intention of returning.

'Word must have got around about how I felt, because Mr Richards came to see me. He asked me what my future was, and I just didn't know what to say. I was quaking in my shoes, but eventually I told him that I could see little point in coming back. To my surprise, he said that if I didn't come, he would travel to Ireland and fetch me back!'

Encouraged by such faith, O'Neill returned to England a matter of weeks later, spent two months in the stables and began race-riding again in September, with spectacular results. 'My first four rides were all winners. I became junior champion that season, with 38 winners, and lost my complete riding allowance. I knew then that I was on my way, and I have never had any more doubts about the job. But at that time, I certainly had no illusions about it either—I wanted to be good, but scarcely thought about being the best. I just thought how lucky I was to be making my living this way.'

In another contrast with Francome, O'Neill has never been retained by a trainer. The retainers in steeplechasing are for relatively small money when compared to those offered on the flat, and unless, like Francome with Fred Winter, you are guaranteed rides on a string of likely winners, the freelance path is often the best. 'While I was young,' O'Neill explains, 'I wanted to get around all the yards in the north, get to know all the trainers and, hopefully, get a choice of rides. Then it was up to me—if I chose the wrong ones, I would flop. Thankfully, it hasn't worked out like that yet.'

On any average winter day, O'Neill will leave his Cumbrian cottage, his wife Sheila and his baby daughter Louise, in the cold grey light before dawn, and will be on horseback by 7.30 a.m. He will have grabbed a cup of tea and a slice of toast on his way to this riding-out session which, despite its uncivilised timing, provides bread-and-butter for the jockeys and is accepted as part of the job. I even had the impression that O'Neill enjoyed it.

Depending on the racing venue for the day, O'Neill will return after two hours or so, change, drink another cup of tea, then, in all probability, meet his north-western neighbour Ron Barry. These two share the driving through the season whenever they are heading the same way, and, through this habit, stave off some of the boredom which inevitably afflicts the jockeys on their motorway marathons.

O'Neill drives an Audi and reckons to add 70,000 miles to the clock each jumping season. 'You get sick of driving sometimes,' he says. 'But I get by, thanks to my tapes. Country and western music mainly, by Irish bands of course.'

Like most riders, Jonjo aims to arrive at the course with an hour to spare before his first race. 'I like to sit quietly for ten minutes or so, just settling down and thinking, before I have to get into my kit. Some jockeys get nervous at this point, particularly before the big rides, but I can't say I ever suffer. I get keyed up, certainly, but not frightened like some do.'

We were standing next to the final fence on Southwell's chase course, now, and I could readily appreciate why anyone might be frightened. Two horses hit the fence and capsized, hurling their jockeys over them like discarded rag dolls. They landed face downwards on the mud, momentarily still, and as I turned to pass comment, O'Neill had gone. He was running across the course towards one of the prostrate figures, his friend Barry. The ambulance men beat him to the body, turned him over to reveal a face heavily smudged with red and brown, then helped him to his feet. He immediately slid once more to the floor, his eyes bulging, dizziness dominant.

It was the end of the day for Ron Barry, and as he was led off, ironically past the winner's enclosure to the ambulance room, O'Neill confirmed: 'Everything's great in this game as long as you are fit and winning. But if you get a lot of falls, and everyone does at some time, you feel like jacking it all in and doing something more sensible.'

O'Neill does not claim to have been unlucky with injuries, but his personal casualty list is not unimpressive: six months out with a broken leg, three months with broken vertebrae in his back, two months each with broken wrist and arm, plus fractures in his nose, chest, ribs, toes and fingers. Concussion, not to mention the regular minor bruising and scraping, he accepted as normal routine.

The worst falls of all, he confessed, were those which occurred at the front of a large and bunched field. 'If I know I am coming off, because the horse has made a mistake, several things flash through my mind. I try to fall properly, then, if there is time, get out of the path of the following horses.'

'If they are too close, I get myself into as small and tight a ball as possible. Then I say to myself, "Please God, don't let them get me." '

Apart from the inevitability of the occasional fall and attendant pain, the greatest frustration in O'Neill's riding life is the repetitive accusation that he overuses his whip. Many racing experts had expressed such a view and, days before I spoke to him, former champion Terry Biddlecombe had said as much on television. Jonjo was not pleased.

'I raise my stick high, which gives people that impression,' he explains. 'But I don't hit the horses as many times as people think I do from the stand—and, at nine stone, I can't hit them very hard anyway.

'It upsets me that so many accuse me of knocking horses about, because I love the animals as much as I love the sport. I never punish a horse when I know he cannot go any faster, and in any case, I rarely use my whip before the second last fence. At that point, if I'm in the race with a chance, of course I use the stick. I've got a rhythm, and if I let it go, and drop the whip, the horse will think he has done his bit and pack up. Perhaps nobody else rides in this style—but I can't help that.'

More than once, in his younger days, O'Neill was called before the stewards to defend himself against allegations of using the stick to excess. 'Maybe I did give them too much in those days,' he concedes. 'But the stewards have come to know me, and my style, and I've had no further trouble. The point is, I can—and frequently do on certain horses—ride just as well without my stick.'

O'Neill's services were in such demand during the 1979–80 season that there were many days when he rode in every race on the card. It was, I suggested, an exhausting business, particularly with the long drive home to follow.

'I very rarely feel physically tired at night,' he said. 'But the fatigue comes more from the fact that I have to go home and spend the evening on the phone to trainers. Mentally, I just want to collapse by that time, and I frequently fall asleep in my chair. I go to bed before ten most nights.'

A non-smoking teetotaller, O'Neill gets his kicks from his riding and his family. But, on the day when I spoke to the man at the top of the trade, I found it disturbingly ironic that 19-year-old Jonathan Haynes—who had ridden his first winner less than a fortnight earlier—was being rushed to Nottingham hospital. His mount in the Southwell selling hurdle had hit the third last, somersaulted three times and landed, dead, on the hapless Haynes. The rider had broken his back and cracked his ribs. He was still partly paralysed, his career over.

6 Owners and amateurs

Jeff King is renowned for two things in the racing world. It is universally agreed that he is one of the finest horsemen in the game. It is also agreed that he is a man who speaks his mind, whatever the cost.

His reputation as a quite brutally blunt personality has led some people to believe he may well have achieved greater success through an attitude of diplomacy. King does not entirely agree. What he does concede is that his manner, and unequivocal honesty, has upset certain people along the way—and that a large proportion of those to take offence have been owners.

Some jockeys to whom I spoke were openly uncomplimentary about owners as a general breed. One highly successful rider answered in one word when I asked him whether he disliked any facet of a jockey's life ... 'owners'. King takes a more moderate line. The majority of owners he has met are very decent people, he says. But there are others ...

The owners are the jockeys' employers. They pay the riding fees, they hand out the percentages to winning riders and, of course, they finance the entire operation of keeping the horse in a decent stable. Without owners and their money, there would be no jockeys, so perhaps it is not entirely surprising that a good deal of Victorian servility still exists when the two meet. Most jockeys still touch their cap, many call their owner 'sir'—and a good deal will say nothing against a horse to its owner, whatever their private view. Jeff King, however, refuses to conceal his feelings.

There are countless tales of Jeff telling an owner, in no uncertain fashion, exactly what he thought of his animal. It is known throughout racing, and a regular conversation piece when his name is mentioned. Many believe, and have always believed, that he should change his approach. But he won't.

'I am probably too honest for my own good. I accept that, and have never thought any differently. But it is the way I am made, and I shall always be that way. If a horse is quite obviously useless, and not going to improve, I will say as much to his owner whether he wants to hear it or not.

'A lot of jockeys take the soft way out and give their owners a lot of flannel. Some owners even prefer it that way. Rather than be told the truth, they seem quite happy to be led along in a fantasy world which is going to dent their wallet at the expense of their ego.

'I see no point in conning them. In the short term, by telling an owner he has a bad horse, I might be doing myself out of two or three rides. But that is not going to break me—and, presuming my judgement is right, the horse would never win a race anyway.

'This attitude has made me unpopular in certain quarters, I know. It may also have cost me some winning rides through owners refusing to have me on their horses again. But I don't worry about it. The sort of people who are going to be offended by honesty are the sort I would not want as friends anyway. And the sort of horses that they own are unlikely to make me champion jockey!

'Over a long career, one is bound to have a share of ups and downs. It happens in any business partnership—and I have certainly had my clashes, with both owners and trainers. But surely the important point is that I am still riding for the same trainers who employed me 15 years ago.

'People have always said that I upset people. I'm not deaf to their comments. But I don't think of myself as either a fiery or an unreasonable person. By being quite honest, the only people I can upset are the fools who want to be flannelled. I don't regret being the way I am, nor would I want to change anything I have done. If I changed just to please everyone, I would no longer be my own man.'

The jockey's involvement with an owner begins indirectly, when he is put up to ride his horse, and continues in person when they meet in the parade ring before the race and in the winners' enclosure, or more often outside it, afterwards. At all three stages, says King, the good owners are distinguishable from the bad.

'The majority will leave the booking of jockeys to their trainer, although in smaller yards without a retained rider, owners tend to have more influence in choosing. Some are very definite about who should ride their horse and while, in certain cases, this is naturally a good thing as rider and horse get on well, it can be taken to unhealthy extremes.

'Certain owners will not go outside the top dozen jockeys, whatever the circumstances. Even if their horse only needs a gentle ride round, without a chance or a thought of winning, they won't be happy unless a Francome or O'Neill is put up. Because of this, stable-lads, some of them very promising, find it hard to make any progress as jockeys.

'Peter Bailey, who retained me for a few years, has a very able lad in Len Griffiths. But because a good deal of his owners have this big-name complex, Peter has great difficulty giving Len rides. In many cases, he would give the horses a better ride than anyone else because he has schooled them and got to know them well. But he is in his late twenties now, and is past the stage of trying to make the grade.

'In the parade ring, most owners are quite comfortable to talk to. They enjoy a laugh and a joke and will only exchange brief opinions on the race ahead. Others can talk about nothing but their horse, and a few are plainly on edge.

'Those who the jockeys find objectionable are the ones who try to dictate the way the race should be run, when in reality they know very little about the game.

'After the race, I always try to have a word with the owner, although if I'm riding in the next and have to rush to change my colours, the owner sometimes doesn't arrive at the horse in time. I am honest, as I've already said, and in return I expect the owner to accept my version of the race.

'Unfortunately, there are some who make the jockey a scapegoat for failure. Again, the trouble comes from those who don't know what they are talking about but like to make it seem that they do. Thankfully, such owners are few and far between, and the great majority are super people.'

Peter Hopkins is a successful owner, and undoubtedly qualifies among the 'super people' to whom King refers. He is a burly man with a friendly face and a manner to match. He has a host of amusing stories and a passion for racing rivalled only by his enthusiasm for cricket.

Hopkins, who has a lucrative tour operating business, owns a string of ten horses—some of them exclusively, mostly in shares—and the pleasure costs him a staggering sum of money.

Despite the fact that his horses are among the most successful in steeplechasing, including Jack Madness and Lumen, and that most of them are trained by Josh Gifford, there are no guarantees in racing. Hopkins, however, takes victory modestly, defeat magnanimously ... and continues to love the life.

He is from a mining background in the Rhondda Valley and, as a boy, was frequently taken to racing at Chepstow and to point-to-point meetings by his father and uncle. When he first owned a horse, his ambition was simply to win a race ... any race. With that achieved, in a minor selling hurdle at Devon and Exeter, his sights were switched to bigger targets. And they are still set high.

Despite all that, Hopkins is not the bombastic type of owner who makes himself so objectionable to jockeys. On the contrary, when I put it to him that owners were not jockeys' favourite people, he nodded in wry agreement.

'A lot of people in this game are very slow to praise talent and effort, very quick to complain about a mistake. The jockey is frequently the one who suffers.

'I realise there are some owners who give us a bad name with the jockeys, men who love to blame the rider for everything that goes wrong. There are, naturally, cases when a failure is the fault of the

Liberally peppered with mud, Jonjo O'Neill exchanges opinions with trainer Gordon Richards on his walk back to the weighing-room.

Bob Davies looks more anxious than his owners as he chats in the parade ring.

jockey, but there are some who make him the scapegoat every time—
and these are normally the owners who know little or nothing about
racing.

'In my case, Josh makes all the decisions. As the trainer, he is the
professional. He knows far more about it than I do, so I leave
everything to him. He will select the jockey and decide how the race
should be run. If I have different ideas, I voice them to him before the
race—not afterwards, as an excuse for failure.

'At the end of a race, I always want to know exactly what a jockey
thinks,' says Hopkins, who added one or two ripe reminiscences of
being told just what Jeff King thought of his horses in years gone by.

'I sometimes feel that a jockey should have ridden a certain race
differently. But where is the point in ranting on about it? The jockey is
the man in charge on the course—he is far more experienced and far
better placed than I am.'

Hopkins ended with the sort of tribute which might increase his
already high popularity with the jockey breed. 'I have a lot of
admiration for them. They are the stars in the part of racing which is
still a sport, as opposed to the industry which flat racing has become.
Jump jockeys have got to be brave. They have got to be real men.'

Jim Wilson is tall for a jockey, heavy even for a jump rider. He has a
long, slightly sad and strikingly emaciated face, and when not in the
saddle he is rarely seen without his pipe. He is extremely popular and
he is an amateur—two things which don't always mix in the world of
steeplechasing jockeys. Next to owners, amateurs rate highly on their
list of complaints.

There was little, if any, muttering in the weighing-room when Jim,
or Mr A. J. Wilson to give him his riding name, scored on two virtual
outsiders for trainer Peter Bailey at Leicester on January 5. Beyond the
unavoidable pangs of envy occasioned by the fact that the rides were not
theirs, the professionals could not have been more pleased.

If, however, the winning rides had been taken by some other
amateur than Wilson, the reaction may easily have been quite different.

Jeff King, who not only finished behind one of Wilson's winners on a
more fancied horse but had the galling experience of having ridden the
successful animal earlier in the season, explained the anomaly.

'There are two sorts of amateurs in this job. Jim Wilson belongs to
the type who ride for fun and have no intention of turning professional.
Nobody minds that attitude at all. But there is a certain resentment
among jockeys against the riders who graduate, quite deliberately, from
amateur to full professional.

'I feel, and I am not alone in the view, that these riders are coming in
through the back door and having two bites at the cherry. If they don't
make the grade, they can always go back to their outside business,

69

whereas the jockeys who have slogged their way through an apprenticeship and contested rides and winners the hard way have no such escape. If they flop, they start again from scratch.

'A good deal of leading riders, past and present, did begin as amateurs. It doesn't make me like them any less, but I do feel the system is wrong.'

The system spawned another entry for that category early in the 1979–80 season when Peter Scudamore, son of the famous Michael, turned professional at the request of the stewards—because he was taking too many rides from the men who earned their living by them.

Scudamore had worked in an estate agent's office in Stow-on-the-Wold before moving up the road to become assistant trainer to David Nicholson. An intelligent 21-year-old with two A-Levels from Belmont Abbey School, Scudamore had always yearned to follow his father, and his style and success during his first full season is difficult to question.

Nevertheless, in the opinion of King and several of his colleagues: 'Peter would not have got so many rides early in his career if he had been a professional.' The owners, you see, save money on an amateur rider ...

Jim Wilson is not blind to the resentments of the pros, and neither does he dispute their reasoning. It is in deference to such a view that, in his own words: 'I try not to ride just anything.'

'I rarely exceed 150 rides a season. I know that some of the professionals feel that their living is being affected by amateurs, and I am also permanently aware that the stewards would not tolerate my riding many more.

'They have seen me twice, over the years, but I have managed to avoid a complete ultimatum. If it came to the crunch and they told me I must turn professional or pack up, I would fight it very strongly.

'I am 29 now, and I don't see myself as a threat to anyone. I would like to go on riding for three or four more years, but my aim is to train. Turning professional at this stage would simply not be worthwhile from anyone's viewpoint.'

Wilson spent two years in France as an assistant trainer, and also a period in Ireland, before he even appeared as a race-rider. Then Fred Winter, who is married to Wilson's aunt, used his influence to persuade David Nicholson to give him a job in his yard. In four years with 'The Duke', he rode a good deal of winners, and reflects on that as the only period in his life when it fleetingly occurred to him to become a pro.

He also married Melinda around that time, and the two of them now run a very successful equine pool in Cheltenham where, among those visiting for rest and swimming, has been the great flat horse Ela-Mana-Mou.

Those two winners at Leicester brought Wilson within three of his career century. 'That,' he says, 'has always been an ambition of mine. For any amateur to ride 100 winners can't be bad. Other than that, I would love to have a winner at Liverpool in the National meeting.'

What he does look forward to in retirement is an end to the daily weight worries. 'To do anything less than 10st. 10lbs., I have got to waste. I may look thin, but I'm heavy-boned and have always had to work to keep my weight down. If I know I am going to have to do 10 stone 4, I will cut food right down to the minimum for two or three days before the race. I might use the sauna the night before, and then put on a sweat jacket to work in the stables during the morning.'

Listening to such a description, I could only wonder why anyone should want to subject themselves to such torture ... let alone to do it all as an amateur.

7 Planning and wasting

Even the most abstemious often forego their principles at Christmas. Diets are temporarily discarded, the bathroom scales furtively hidden from view until the feasting is over. Jockeys, however, can afford no such frivolity.

In 1979, there was a three-day break from racing—and then eight scheduled meetings on Boxing Day. For many riders, obliged to maintain their regular minimum weight, there could be no festive blowout.

Jeff King was luckier than most. Booked to ride in the major meeting at Kempton on Boxing Day, he was not obliged to get below 11st., 10lb. above his best weight. His Christmas Day house party of relatives and friends totalled nine, and he was able to enjoy it without too much stinting.

In the past, however, it has often been different. 'There have been many years when Christmas has been marred by the thought of racing the following day, and the knowledge that I could not eat a proper dinner without ruining my weight.

'For that reason, the Christmas festivities probably mean less to jockeys than to most other people. This year, however, I had decided that I would not take a "light ride" unless the horse had a real chance. I saw no point in spoiling the day for myself and the family just to trail in on a bad animal.'

Over the other side of the M4 motorway at Lambourn, champion jockey John Francome was also tucking into turkey without fear. But his meal was tainted with both pain and disappointment. The pain came from the shoulder he had dislocated at Chepstow three days earlier; the disappointment from the fact that Border Incident, one of his best rides, would be running without him at Kempton. 'I would much rather have to go without Christmas dinner and be able to ride him,' said Francome.

Another aspect of Christmas for the jockeys is the difficulties it presents in the planning of rides. With 12 meetings over two days, resources of riders were inevitably stretched, and the top jockeys were invariably left with a choice between rides at a number of meetings.

Jonjo O'Neill could undoubtedly have ridden at any one of the eight

Boxing Day courses had he made himself available. Pleasant though it may be to feel oneself in constant demand, O'Neill points out that there are aspects of the situation which he does not relish.

'Sometimes the hardest part of this job can be the decisions. I hate them, because I so dislike upsetting people—and that cannot be avoided when you have to make a choice between different horses, different trainers.

'I plan my rides on the weekly Racing Calendar. My wife, Sheila, takes messages from trainers and I also have an answering machine installed on my telephone. But every night, the buck stops with me. I have to make my choice—and I try to put it off as long as possible.

'Reading form is an enjoyable pastime to me. I get a kick out of the whole thing, and I like to think I am not a bad judge when it comes to deciding which of two or three offered mounts to accept.

'But there will always be occasions when I get it wrong, when the other horse wins and I come trailing in behind it. That is a very irritating experience. Even worse, in my view, is when you have gone through all the bother of choosing horses, you turn up at the track and the weather has forced an abandonment. There can be nothing worse than never knowing whether you made the right decision or not.'

Francome spends most Sundays attempting to organise his rides for the week ahead. It is a task, he says, which will often defeat him with its futility.

'Fred Winter alone has 60 horses in his yard, and might have several declared at different meetings on the same day, waiting to see how the opposition looks and what the ground is like. I try to plan ahead, but I can never do it with any certainty.'

Unlike the freelance O'Neill, Francome is retained by Winter, and must ride his horses in preference to anything else. For all its benefits, this can create extra headaches when booking outside rides.

'I don't think I get as many outside rides as I might, but the reason could well be that other trainers assume I will already have a mount and don't consider it worthwhile approaching me. I tend to accept rides wherever I can, and then get off them if I have to. But I don't like messing trainers about—I'm probably a bit soft like that. I know they have a difficult time, especially if they haven't got any retained riders.

'To help me in future, I keep an account of every horse I ride, and how it performed, noting little things like whether it pulled right or left, what sort of going it likes etc. Small things maybe, but they are tips which help.'

Jeff King makes no conscious effort to plan any farther ahead than the following day. He also differs from a high proportion of his colleagues in that he will never approach a trainer to offer himself for a ride.

'Having been retained by Bob Turnell for so long, I know he would never have thought much of a jockey who phoned up to push himself. But, while I always wait for the trainers to come to me, I realise a lot of jockeys do take the initiative—and, in flat racing, even the likes of Lester Piggott do it.

'A lot of a jockey's time is spent on the phone and it can become tedious. But it keeps you going to think what it would mean if the phone ever stopped ringing. Even as a freelance, I have trainers who give me a lot of rides—and they naturally take preference in my plans. I have often turned down three or four rides at another meeting to ride a couple for, say, Ron Smyth or Verley Bewicke.

'However hard you may try to be fair, there are always one or two trainers who get ratty when you can't ride their horses. For the jockey, it can become a question of choosing who to upset!'

The weather, so often a depressant in a jockey's life, just occasionally works in one's favour. It had happened for King on December 28.

Christmas, far from being fluffily white and festive, had at first been treacherously icy, and then torrentially wet. By Friday 28, much of the country was being affected, or at least threatened, by flood conditions. Stratford's meeting was still on when the groundsman inspected on Thursday night, but 12 hours later the only method of testing the course was by boat. The Avon had burst its banks with spectacular results. One jockey booked to ride there phoned the course office, where a worried and reluctant official declined to pass verdict on whether the day's sport would go ahead. When asked by the rider for the condition of the track, he was forced to concede that racing was unlikely 'as it's under a foot of water ... but don't take my word for it, please!'

Things were not so clear-cut at Fontwell, where King was scheduled to ride, but the meeting was eventually abandoned after a morning inspection. King now moved fast. He had been obliged to turn down the ride on Tim Forster's Pencraig at the Newbury meeting due to previous Fontwell bookings. Now he went back to Forster and was immediately substituted for the amateur, Tim Thomson-Jones.

It was the sort of break King had not enjoyed previously this season. Pencraig, several lengths behind the favourite at the last fence, was driven to victory by an inspired piece of riding, ending 16 winner-less days for King since the same horse had come home first at Worcester.

The following day's papers featured the race heavily, lauding King's vintage efforts in words and pictures. Though not a man unduly swayed by press criticism, Jeff was undoubtedly relieved. 'When you have a long spell without a winner, you sometimes start to worry subconsciously. It's a good feeling to end the run by driving one home, proving that you still have the ability and the urge.'

What he did not know at the time was that 29 days were to pass before he set foot in the winners' enclosure again.

If the weather was King's samaritan on that occasion, the deed was balanced four days later. Booked to ride the fancied Prince Rock for trainer Peter Bailey, who had at one time retained him as stable jockey, King decided to forego all New Year's Eve celebrations.

'I believed Prince Rock had a great chance of winning at Cheltenham, and there was no way I wanted to upset my weight with a few drinks. I suppose I could have gone out and drunk nothing, but to me that is worse than staying at home. So I shut my mind to New Years' Eve and sat in while my wife went out with some friends.'

The abstinence was all for nothing. Cheltenham's meeting was abandoned at 7.30 a.m. on New Years' Day, while much of the population was waking up with hangovers and King was feeling soberly fresh.

Prince Rock finally found a race on January 5 in the rich Anthony Mildmay-Peter Cazalet Memorial Chase at Sandown Park. King was again on board, but, on a course which failed to suit his needs, Prince Rock was a disappointing sixth and King was left to continue one of the leanest sequences in his 21 years as a jockey.

John Thorne

In any other walk of life, a perfectly healthy man of 53 who voluntarily confined himself to a diet of boiled eggs, steamed fish and salads, deprived himself of alcohol and condemned himself to losing 2lb. a day in a health farm, might be considered eccentric at best. In National Hunt racing, the mere mention of such sacrifices brings immediate smiles of recognition. The man in question has to be John Thorne.

Years ago, there were many like him. When the Corinthian spirit was rife and sport was just a bit of fun, his deeds and his determination would have attracted little attention. These days, however, the age of professionalism dictates that Mr Thorne is a little bit special.

He lives in the Warwickshire village of Chesterton, which nestles quietly between Stratford-upon-Avon and Warwick. His profession is farming—365 acres of arable land and beefstock—but his passion is horses: owning them, breeding them, training them and riding them, as an amateur, of course.

This season his name, whenever mentioned, was coupled with that of one particular horse ... Spartan Missile. A potentially brilliant eight-year-old, 'Missile' was being aimed at both the Cheltenham Gold Cup and the Grand National. Thorne intended to ride his horse in both races—and damn the discomfort. For the National, you see, Spartan Missile had been allocated a weight of 11st. 9lb. to carry, and that is approximately 19 pounds below John's regular weight.

No 53-year-old loses 19 pounds easily, and Thorne freely confessed that the chore of getting weight off is, to him, a hateful business. But his conviction that he could do it never wavered.

Five weeks before the National, I spoke with him at Kempton Park. We were in the owners' and trainers' bar, for which John qualified on both counts and I on neither, and he was sipping champagne. It was, he said, his first drink for several weeks, the justification being a horse he had bred and owned having just won a hurdle event. He looked trim and fit, but the truth of it was that he still pushed the scales up to 12st. 7lb. Almost another stone to lose.

'I shall make it,' he said confidently. 'Whenever this problem arises, I book myself into a health farm for a week and reckon to shed two pounds a day there. It's far easier than trying to starve at home, where there are so many temptations.

'When my daughters were still living at home, it was even worse. They always seemed to be tucking into something while I was around. I am a compulsive chocolate eater, you see, and unless I take a firm grip of myself, I can very quickly undo a great deal of hard work.

'Even now that the girls have moved out and are both married, it isn't easy. Food and drink are pleasures to me. Cutting them down to such an extent comes very hard, and I find I have to take myself off somewhere at meal times. My wife, Wendy, is not very keen on the idea of me starving myself, nor, come to that, on the fact that I still ride at all. But she knows she has no option, so she is tolerant and helpful when it comes to keeping food away from me.'

If it still seemed a strange way for a middle-aged man to be behaving, John's explanation was disarmingly simple. 'Steeplechasing is great fun to me. I love every side of it, but particularly the actual riding. And Aintree is the pinnacle. Riding around that course gives me the greatest thrill imaginable.'

In 1979, Thorne had ridden an unforgettable race at Aintree, taking Spartan Missile to victory in the Foxhunters' Chase, twenty years after he won the event on the first generation of Missile's family. The horse was now clearly a source of affection and dedication from the entire Thorne family, and John was honest enough to admit: 'We get too involved. It's so easy to become carried away with a particular horse, when you have been responsible for him from the breeding stage right through to racing.'

The Thorne family history is surprisingly blank when it comes to racing. 'Most of my earlier family were regular soldiers,' John explains, 'but I was always interested enough to ride, and I contested point-to-point races for years.'

During the war, Thorne served in the Sixth Airborne Regiment, and was involved in the operation to cross the Rhine, which perhaps helps to explain his relish for the danger of Aintree's fences. Following that, he spent two years serving in Palestine 'when it was like Northern Ireland is today.'

Even then, staying slim was a problem. 'I was 22 when I came out of the army, and I weighed 13st. 7lb., two stone heavier than when I went in. I had to box as a heavyweight in the army, but I was so short that I was always outreached and outpunched.'

John's stud at Chesterton comprises four stallions plus eight mares to breed from. The horses, he says, take up more of his time than they should, because they provide one-third of his income. But he is unlikely to take any notice of his conscience.

Despite his irregular appearances in the saddle, mainly confined to hunter chases these days, John has endured his share of falls and injuries. 'My nerve is still good. One always gets tense before a race, and things are probably not right otherwise. But I have never been frightened. What I will say is that, after a particularly bad fall, I am always pleased to get the next one over with. The nagging feeling at the back of the mind suggests the next one may be your last, so it is a relief when you get through it without too much damage.'

Among Thorne's more serious injuries are a broken leg, broken collarbones, and a broken back—the latter of which very nearly stopped his riding days for good, and contributed to a touching family tale.

'The fall occurred at Leicester, and I was told by one doctor that I should never ride again. Fortunately, I sought a second opinion which was more to my liking, but the fact remained that I was incarcerated in a plaster cast for some time, and someone else had to be found to ride our horses, particularly Indenelia, who had won some very good hurdle races.

'My son Nigel was 16 at the time, and one day he came to his mother and asked who was going to ride Indenelia while I was laid up. Wendy replied that she didn't know, and to her surprise Nigel said: "I think I would like to."

'It was a major step, of course, but I was willing to give him a try. On the day that he was to ride, one of his school governors drove Nigel to the course. I had had a word with David Nicholson, who was also riding in the race, asking him to look after Nigel if he could. Sure enough, David chatted to him and rode down to the start with him.

'As I was still in plaster, I had to spend a good bit of the afternoon lying down on the back seat of the car. But I came out for the race, and was helped into a seat in the stand. I have never been as nervous as I was before and during that race, but to our delight, Nigel came to the last level with David Nicholson's mount. They fought a ding-dong battle all the way up the straight, and Nigel got Indenelia home by a neck.'

That was son Nigel's first racing winner. He went on to ride several more and, at the age of 18, was working and riding for trainer Tom Jones at Newmarket, when he was killed in a car crash.

John's daughters, Diana—now married to top trainer Nicky

Henderson—and Jane were the first and second women riders respectively to win over jumps, in 1976. They both still ride now, but with no great frequency, and it is a poignant fact that the loss of his son has indirectly kept John Thorne in the saddle.

'Nigel was almost ready to take over riding all our horses,' he says. 'And I was set to take a back seat. I certainly would not be riding now, not thinking of riding Spartan Missile in the 'National, if he was still alive.'

8 Good breaks and bad

It was at Taunton on January 24 that King struck his lowest ebb of the winter. He had four rides that day. Two were well fancied yet failed to finish in the first three; the other two came in third. Totting up, that made a total of 27 days, or 29 mounts, since King's last winner, on Pencraig just after Christmas.

Jeff has been riding too long to become emotional or distraught over such runs, but even he could not accept this one without traces of depression. Those friends who asked after him at the races were treated to a shrug, a grimace and 'I'd be a lot better if I could ride a winner.'

He avoids the subject of racing at home, and never burdens his family with his worries. But his wife, Maureen, was only too well aware of his anxiety, and as keen as Jeff for that elusive winner.

The Taunton card looked promising but turned sour. Twice, as the field raced down the back straight for the last time, he believed he would win, only for his mount to 'blow up' on the turn for home. The most disappointing ride of all was on Irish Shamrock, favourite for the two-mile, three-furlong Chase, yet so far back at the finish that the stewards held an enquiry at which King had to explain his riding tactics.

From the start of the day, Jeff had insisted that the race was too short for a horse who, in his view, ran far more effectively over three miles. Events appeared to prove him right. But the owners were unhappy and trainer Nick Gaselee, for whom King had ridden so often during the season, followed their wishes. Jeff lost the ride. Irish Shamrock went on to win two three-mile races in the next three weeks, ridden by Richard Evans.

'Some trainers, Nick among them, reckon I don't try as hard as I might,' he said later. 'The only truth in that view is the fact that I won't kill a horse to get him into fifth place rather than seventh—I just don't see the point. But when you are having this sort of run, everyone is happy to think the worst.

'I hear the knockers everywhere. "Kingy is finished," they say. "He doesn't give them a good ride these days." I'd be lying if I said I enjoyed hearing such comments, but they don't hurt me because I am always my own biggest critic. I know when I've ridden a bad race and I will give myself a mental bollocking for it. But I also know that I am not over the top. In my own mind, I don't think I am any worse a rider now than I was five years ago.

'I am not made like Graham Thorner, who would never accept second best and finally quit when things were going badly. Any pain that I feel through failure is eased by knowing I've only got two or three more years to go, anyway. Losing rides now is an annoyance, but it won't break me.'

Fontwell

The voice at the other end of the telephone was a little scornful, a little insistent. 'Yes,' he said wearily, 'today's meeting is definitely on.' And so it was, although how and why racing took place on the Fontwell Park swamp on February 6 must be one of the mysteries of the jumping season.

It was 9.30 a.m. when I made that call to the course office. Ninety minutes later, when I set off for the 60-mile drive from Berkshire, the rain which had put every sporting event in doubt for days, had begun again. It fell incessantly, and ever more heavily, as I wound through the lanes towards the charming Fontwell course, sandwiched between Chichester and Arundel just up from the Sussex coast.

The car park attendant, one of that hardy breed in his job who wear the same clothes and same expression whatever the weather, and always seem to have information to impart, told me that there had been an inspection at 11.30 a.m. and the meeting was still on. I found it difficult to believe.

I squelched my way across the course, the car park being inconveniently placed on the far side from the stands, and wondered what it would look like in three hours time. A solitary, and somewhat elderly groundsman was prodding the mud half-heartedly with a fork as if he thought the floods might miraculously subside into the prong-holes.

John Buckingham, the jockey's valet, had arrived early and been told that one more shower would see the meeting abandoned. As it had rained non-stop since then, and showed no sign of relenting, John was entitled to feel bewildered, not to mention chagrined as his job now entailed looking after several dozen men who were about to coat themselves in mud.

Amazingly, not one horse was withdrawn from the six-race programme. Almost equally surprising was the fact that no injuries occurred either to horses or jockeys.

Jeff King was at first mildly amused by the conditions, which he described as 'diabolical—among the worst I've ever ridden in', but he was less than deliriously happy about the effect on his first mount of the meeting, a favourite in the selling hurdle which steadfastly refused to gallop through the mud and eventually had to be pulled up.

Almost without exception, the horses were finishing in a state of complete fatigue, the jockeys not a lot better. More than one rider elected to walk his mount over the last few yards to the finishing post and turn him round immediately. Mud liberally splashed the face of every jockey except the few who led from start to finish. King himself was one who chose to wear extra protection in the form of tan-coloured mackintosh breeches over his normal jockey strip. Those who did not invariably returned with their white breeches so wet that those in the stands could see through them.

Before going out for his second and last ride, on a horse quaintly named Slippery Dick, King left none of the officials within the weighing-room in any doubt about his view of the conditions. Nevertheless, he drove Slippery Dick into the lead from the start of the $3^1/_4$-mile chase, the day's longest race, and kept him there to win by two lengths.

Returning to the weighing-room in good spirits, but with his opinion on the track unaltered, he declared: 'If this is racing, I'm Muhammad Ali.' A new nickname could instantly have been born.

With the martyr's marathon finally over, the marshy parade ring emptied and the majority of spectators squelched their way home. I picked my way across the bog that was once a grassy race-course and wondered that my ruined pair of shoes was among the afternoon's most serious casualties.

The day was not without a twist. While King had been riding a winner in Sussex, 21-year-old Peter Scudamore had been in Lancashire to ride Fred Rimell's horses at Haydock Park. His first mount was Brian's Venture, which King had taken to third place at Nottingham ten days earlier. This time he was fourth, and finished tired. Scudamore, the rising young star tagged by many the 'discovery' of the jumping season, pulled him up quickly, then felt a sharp pain as another horse cannoned into his side. He returned to the unsaddling enclosure slumped forward over his horse's head, his leg broken in two places.

For Peter Scudamore, the party was over. Just as the exciting climax to his first full season was approaching, so this precarious existence chose the moment to remind him of its perils.

He was carried into the weighing-room by his father, while his mother looked on. The leg was plastered in a local hospital, and he was allowed to be driven to his parents' home that night. It was there that I met him, the following morning.

The Scudamores
It is all very well for jockeys to dismiss injuries as 'things that happen'. They frequently do so with a glibness born of resignation to the inevitable. Such philosophical acceptance, however, never comes so

easily to a mother. Mary Scudamore is perhaps an extreme case, but it is hardly surprising. Her husband rode for two decades until narrowly surviving with his senses intact from a hideous kicking by a horse; her son had discovered the harsh side of racing when a freak accident broke his leg just as his professional career was burgeoning. Now, to cap it all, her pretty teenage daughter is impatiently seeking race-rides.

The face of 'Mum' is kindly, yet bears almost constant signs of anxiety. She frequently attends racing when any one of her family is involved, yet for her the whole affair is cruel masochism, ended only when they all leave the course undamaged.

As often as not, she finds it impossible even to watch a race when son Peter is riding. She will pace endlessly behind the stands, or even spend the time in the ladies' loo. She likes him to win, of course, but her overwhelming concern is that he comes back fit.

So it was ironic that the injury which ended young Scudamore's noteworthy run of success in 1979 occurred after the finishing post had been passed, and after Mary had heaved her customary sigh of relief.

Brian's Venture was a promising hurdler in the Fred Rimell stable, for which Peter had been riding just a month. In a race of no great class, he had finished a disappointing fourth. With the horse patently tired, Peter pulled up quickly after passing the post. Sam Morshead, whose mount was bearing down fast from behind, yelled at him to hold his course in order to avoid a collision. He did so, but a split second later, another horse thundered into his right side. The excruciating pain which followed told him instantly that this was something serious; in fact what had happened was that the horse's shoulder had hit him, breaking his leg in two places below the knee.

His mother, had actually seen the finish of the race from the stand. 'As usual,' she recalled the next day, 'I thought "Thank God that's over". I was squeezing my way through the crowd as soon as he passed the post. Like many other people, I didn't even see the collision. The first I knew of it was when I reached the unsaddling enclosure and saw Peter come through, leaning forward on his horse's head and looking terrible. Michael helped carry him in and someone said to me that he had broken his leg. I panicked.'

The leg was plastered in a Liverpool hospital. 'The doctor got me talking about football,' says Peter. 'He was on about Liverpool all the time, and I wanted to put a case for Nottingham Forest, the team I follow. But as he had hold of my leg at the time, I thought better of it!' He was allowed to leave that evening, and lay on the back seat of his parents' car as Michael drove him to their isolated, farmhouse home.

It lies on high ground above the River Wye on the Welsh borders. Fifteen horses were resident in Michael's stables—he turned to training when his riding career ended—and it was an unkind irony that one of

Ron Atkins, with colours and tack, on the scales at Windsor before a race, while in the background Graham Thorner holds his head.

Peter Scudamore, one day the fastest-rising star of 1980, the next a nobody again after a broken leg at Haydock.

his few winners in a thus far unrewarding season had been achieved later in the Haydock programme which brought Peter's injury. He can hardly have been in the mood to enjoy it.

There is nothing of the dreamer about Michael. His features are rugged and lined, not only with the advancing years but the lasting scars of his days in—and out—of the saddle. Life has made him a realist, and although he is quietly proud and gratified that his son has chosen a riding career and made something of it, he could never be surprised when the falls caught up with him.

'Don't tell his mother,' he had said, scarcely a month earlier, 'but I know he is going to get hurt at times. It's part of the job.'

'My first thought when this happened,' he told me the next morning, 'was that I had expected something because it had all been going so well for Pete. But then I changed my mind. After all, why should it catch up with him now? Jonjo O'Neill has had three years at the top without a serious injury. It is something which must be accepted, certainly, but not expected.'

Michael's life is generally a contented one, just as his active riding career had always been. He loved the racing, and enjoyed the extracurricular side—the camaraderie, the sociability, the impromptu sessions at a staging-post on the way home from racing. 'I don't believe things are quite the same any more, but then I'm looking at it from a generation apart and I know Pete feels differently.'

'There were some amazing characters riding in my time, and there seemed to be a higher proportion who socialised. Not much of it went on in the bars at the courses, mind, for if a trainer as much as saw you there, he would assume you were out on the booze and blame you for anything that went wrong the next day—it wouldn't matter whether you had only had a glass of lemonade or ten pints of beer!

'I remember two characters called Speck and Stott who went out on the town in London one evening. The evening turned into night, and morning arrived with the revels still going on. So Specky and Stotty did the only thing they could, and arrived at Newbury for the Saturday racing, still in their dinner jackets and bow ties. I'll bet they gave their horses one hell of a ride, too.'

He won the Cheltenham Gold Cup on Linwell in 1957, the Grand National on Oxo two years later. He imagined nothing better than riding for another 15 years or so. But fate had other things in mind for Scudamore senior, and a damp day at Wolverhampton took away his career and might just as easily have taken his life.

'I came off on the flat when my horse slipped,' he recalls, all too vividly. 'As I went down, a passing horse caught me full in the face and chest with his hoof. But it didn't knock me out—I was conscious through it all. I had to sit up on the stretcher, leaning on one elbow, because I was scared that I might choke on the blood that was pouring from my mouth.'

Thankfully, Mary was not present to see this grimmest of racing accidents. When she arrived at the hospital, it was to be told that her husband was suffering from a punctured lung, a jaw broken in two places, a fractured cheekbone, a broken nose and enough lumps and cuts to make him scarcely recognisable. That kick had also taken 90 per cent of the sight from his left eye, an affliction he is still living with today.

Perhaps the most extraordinary thing is that Michael's enthusiasm for racing was not drained. 'They told me I could never ride again,' he relates. 'But I wouldn't believe it. I was determined that this would not stop me leading the life I wanted to. My face was a hell of a mess, though, and the doctors had to put it together again like a jigsaw. Eventually, I accepted their decision, but only because my eye was not good enough to judge fences. It was a terrible wrench, but I am glad I managed to stay in the sport by training.'

It was easy to sense the same dedication and passion in son Peter. He was in a comfortable arm-chair when I arrived at the homely farm-house, his leg resting on a pile of cushions. On the floor at his side lay more than a dozen paperbacks, all by Dick Francis, all thrillers about the racing world, many of them featuring injured jockeys. 'I've read them all before,' he said. 'But they help to pass the time.'

He pushed his hand impatiently through his short, dark hair as he related the saga of the crash, the improbability of it all. 'I had gone two months without a fall of any kind, and I had come not to expect any. I grew cocky about it. Subconsciously, I probably felt I was good enough not to need the luck. Then I had four falls in two weeks—and now this.'

There had been some suggestion of incompetence on the part of the rider whose horse had cannoned into Peter. But he was so lacking in revengeful or resentful feelings that he even refused to name him. What galled him far more was the thought of sitting about for two, maybe three months, while a stack of good rides for the Rimell stable were taken by somebody else—principally, as it turned out, by Jeff King and John Burke. Peter grimaced good-naturedly as he flicked once more through the racing papers and lingered over the rides he might have had that day. In any case, however, the weather had accounted for both the scheduled meetings. 'That is the only consolation.'

Peter's decision to race-ride had dismayed his mother, who probably thought her days of worry and anxiety on chilly racetracks had ended with Michael's retirement. Both parents thought it wise for him to have alternatives, however, so he obtained two 'A' levels at school—where he was deputy head-boy—and then took a job in an estate agent's office in Stow-on-the-Wold, fortuitously the base for David Nicholson's training stables. Most of his early riding work and race-rides were for

Nicholson, until Rimell split with his jockey Colin Tinkler and offered the job to the boy with the fast-flowering reputation. By then, he had shed his amateur status and was devoting himself to racing.

He was strikingly philosophical about his plight, and even managed a chuckle over a somewhat startling coincidence. Peter shares a cottage in the Gloucestershire village of Bourton-on-the-Hill with Alan Webb, another aspiring young jockey. Four days before his Haydock mishap, Webb had suffered a crashing fall at Stratford ... and broken his neck. What is more, a trio of sidelined jockeys is provided by Roy Mangan, who lives just down the road from Scudamore and Webb and shares the same local pub. His season had just been ended by a broken knee. The stuff of which nightmares are made.

While Peter answered frequent calls from wellwishers on the phone placed conveniently next to his chair, and mother fussed over the cushions under his leg, an attractive, fresh-faced blonde girl dismounted in the stable-yard outside. Sister Nicky.

The unity of this family had already struck me, and Nicky only emphasised it. She called her brother 'Scu', her father's racing nickname too, and sat down at his side. She also, incidentally, calls her father 'Bert'. He, in turn, addresses her as 'Doris' ...

Nicky had been riding out that morning, on one of Michael's horses. Nicky wants to be a jockey. Already, she had had two rides on the flat, and one over jumps at Kempton Park, in an amateur's race on January 19. I had seen her after racing that night, radiant with the thrill and satisfaction of completing the course. I had seen Michael and Mary too, both proud but wary, resistant to the impatience of their daughter, who now sought further rides more persistently each day.

'My next race can't come soon enough,' Nicky told me. 'I'm trying to persuade Dad to let me ride a horse of his.' Dad, however, was in no hurry to see his daughter risk her neck again.

'I don't think girls were made for this game,' he said. 'She knows I don't like her riding. She knows, too, that I won't stop her if she wants it badly enough. We must all have ambitions, and I will not stand in her way if this is hers.

'But I worry about her, of course. I jumped every fence with her at Kempton, never took my glasses off her. She rode well and I was delighted for her. But whereas I can accept and enjoy Peter taking the jockey's career, it is different with Nicky. I can't stand the thought of her being knocked about. It's different for girls, isn't it?'

'Doris', I felt, was not likely to stop pestering 'Bert', so more traumatic afternoons undoubtedly lay ahead for the Scudamore family. But I left them in their Herefordshire haven, after being given a superb lunch, with the lasting thought that I had met the sort of people who make steeplechase racing what it is. Honest, passionately involved, and among the friendliest families I have ever known.

One of the anomalies of any serious injury to a jump jockey is that it directly helps one or more of his colleagues. In the case of Peter Scudamore's broken leg, it was King who initially profited by being engaged for several of the Fred Rimell horses which would otherwise have been ridden by the 21-year-old prodigy.

In the fortnight after Scudamore's mishap, King rode eight Rimell horses. Only one, Shaftesbury, was a winner, but several others were placed or ran promisingly. A short-term boost it may have been, but it certainly aided King's prospects of improving what he was now describing as 'my worst season for 20 years'.

Experience has taught him to take nothing for granted in this game, and it was only occasionally through the season that he would visibly and verbally fancy a horse to win. One such occasion was February 22 at Kempton Park.

The previous day at Wincanton he had ridden three Rimell horses. Shaftesbury had won, North Yard finished second and Another Dolly— a possible Grand National ride for him—had returned well after a 16-month rest. But he had fancied none of those as strongly as Brian's Venture, the horse on which Scudamore had met his fate and now due to run in the first hurdle of the card at Kempton.

An expensive horse, he had twice been a beaten favourite, and was cast by many as a disappointment. King never thought so. What is more, he was convinced that Kempton was the right course for him and that this, an open and moderate-class race, was the ideal stage for his maiden victory.

Rain the previous day had not helped, and King arrived early and walked the course, testing the ground and planning his own tactics for the ride, clearly the best of his four that afternoon.

One by one, the other jockeys arrived. The horse boxes were into the car park and unloading their valuables ... but there was no sign of the Rimell box containing Brian's Venture. It never arrived, and the horse was reluctantly withdrawn.

It was a complicated misadventure. The Rimells had just bought a new box, and transferred the tool kit from the old vehicle to the new. So when the old box, carrying Brian's Venture, suffered a puncture on the motorway near Reading, and the driver searched for his spanners to remove the flat tyre, he searched in vain.

Not a man to easily give up on a fancied horse, he then sprinted two miles to the nearest garage, paid £6 deposit for a set of spanners and raced back to the stricken lorry. None of the spanners fitted ...

He returned once more to the garage where, to add insult to injury, the proprietor refused to refund the money. By now, in any event, it was too late. King, fretting at the races no more than 20 miles away, had lost his ride in the most unfortunate manner.

Just to make things considerably worse, and add another minus mark to the season, King was not able to ride when Brian's Venture did run again, at Newbury a week later. Two hundred miles away at Haydock Park, where Drusus had just finished a shattering last in the Embassy Chase Final for which he had once been favourite, King studied the results board. Brian's Venture had won at 6 to 1. Sam Morshead was the rider. Jeff King was less than delighted.

Just across the River Trent, the crowds were starting to file into Nottingham Forest's City ground for the afternoon's First Division match against Middlesborough. By kick-off time, the gate had swelled to almost 30,000. But at the modest, dull-bricked and somewhat discouraging racecourse, about ten per cent of that number turned up for what was billed as racing's 'Match of the Day'.

It was the clash of Beacon Light, who had won all of six starts as a steeplechaser, and Drusus, a six-year-old horse of considerable promise. Only three others ran, and all were discounted. This, said the bookies at least, was a two-horse race.

Jeff King was to ride Drusus, and the horse represented one of the brighter horizons in this unusually bleak season for him. He had been retained by the owner to ride Drusus for the rest of the season, including at least two rich races. Here, in a £6,000 televised two-mile chase, Drusus was tackling his greatest challenge yet.

Beacon Light is trained by Bob Turnell, King's former employer, and ridden by Andy Turnell, King's good friend but also the man whose arrival in his father's stable virtually ensured that King would end his connections and become a freelance.

During the week leading up to the race, King was dubious about Drusus's chances against such a mighty opponent, so close to more major engagements. But by Saturday morning, as mist hung over the Marlborough Downs and rain slanted insistently across the sky, his apprehensions were transferred to the possibility that the ground may be too heavy for the horse even to run.

Nottingham, however is a 2¹/₂-hour drive from King's home, and the weather there was more clement; dull and cloudy but considerably drier. Drusus would run.

The bookies, following their noses as ever, installed Beacon Light as a heavily odds-on favourite, and Drusus drifted out to 5 to 2. King confessed that he knew only one way to beat the horse, and that was to go on ahead from the start and set a pace that might kill Beacon's awesome finishing speed.

At first, the race went perfectly to plan. Drusus made all the running, it was quickly evident that only Beacon Light could catch him and, as the leader turned to enter the straight for the last time he was still five lengths clear.

Steadily, agonisingly, the inches were stolen back. Four lengths, then three and, as Drusus approached the last fence, it was only two. But by now, Turnell had demanded a good deal of his mount. Just how much did he have left?

We never got to know. King slapped Drusus with his whip, asking him for the final effort at the last fence, but the horse could not or would not respond. He flopped against the obstacle, landed in a nose-dive and shot King out of the saddle, leaving Beacon Light to canter home unchallenged.

King, who had landed head-first but appeared to bounce to his feet, remounted and walked Drusus sadly back to unsaddle. By all appearances he was unharmed by the fall, but even then, his head felt a little groggy and had started to ache.

He completed his second booked ride an hour later, the head feeling considerably worse. At the end of it, he withdrew from his remaining two races, changed back into street clothes and joined the crowd in the stand.

'I always think it is foolish to carry on riding after a bang on the head,' he said. 'This may be no more than a headache, but if I shake it up again it can do no good. The head is our most vulnerable part—and I've only got one.'

The irony here is that Turnell himself took a dreadful tumble in the third race, somersaulted three times on landing and aggravated his persistent neck injury. He too, withdrew from later rides, and was disorientated enough a few minutes later to have completely forgotten he had asked John Francome to deputise.

King had to watch Richard Evans partner Pencraig, on whom he had twice been successful, and was honest enough to admit: 'I hope he doesn't win without me.' In the last event, Sam Morshead deputised on Havon Cool and again King was willing him to lose. He had nothing personal against the jockeys involved; his sentiments were natural self-preservation.

We stopped at Jeff's local for some cigarettes and the landlord remarked wryly that he had been trying to lipread as he watched the fall on television. The landlady, more emotionally, said she had been so upset she had been close to tears.

The headache did not immediately ease. King went to a dinner party that night and fell asleep straight after the meal, waking only after everyone had left. He still felt less than fit on Sunday, and decided not to risk riding the following day. It was only a precaution, but a sensible one.

'What a game this is,' he said. 'We must all be mad—I drive 300 miles to land on my head and ruin my weekend ...'

9 Punting and pulling

The know-all consulted his race-card, glanced up at the jockey board and sagely shook his head. 'Jeff King rides the grey, Haytor Mist,' he announced to his uninformed friend. 'He's a good jockey alright, but they say he stops a lot.'

I did not wait to find out who 'they' might be, nor indeed if know-all and friend decided to forget their prejudice and pile their pound on Haytor Mist. If they did, that was the last they were to see of it—not through any malpractice on King's part but because the poor animal was so weary by the third last fence that he hit it hard and gently subsided to the floor.

This particular episode occurred at Sandown Park on January 5, but it is by no means an unusual conversation to overhear around any parade ring or in any stand. King is no more likely to be the culprit than any other jockey for, in the eyes of many public racegoers, if their horse is beaten the rider must have stopped it.

'Stopping' involves pulling a horse back to prevent it winning or, in most cases, even finishing in the frame. It undoubtedly exists as an occasional though not universal practice in National Hunt and, if the jump jockeys are to be believed, is more prevalent on the flat.

The aim is generally to enter the stopped horse for a later race, in which he will probably run at an attractive enough price for either owner or trainer, often both, to have a sizeable gamble. Not every trainer encourages this; in fact many will have no part of it.

Most jockeys tread carefully around this delicate issue, but one leading rider was frank enough to say: 'If I am asked to stop one, then I will do it. It is just part of the job.' King himself would have been amused and faintly irritated by the Sandown know-all. For as he says: 'You hear a great deal of rubbish talked in the stands on this subject. In many races, you can see one horse run on very strongly to the finish, and the inevitable cry will go up that he was stopped. In fact, it is much more likely that the horse needed an extra half-mile.'

'I do not believe very many get stopped in jump-racing, but now and again a horse will certainly be pulled up, so that the connections can have a punt another day. But the majority of jockeys are not too interested in throwing away a possible winner, because there is little enough money in steeplechasing anyway.

'In my 13 years attached to Bob Turnell's stable, I never rode one horse that was to be stopped—but I rode many under instructions to give them a quiet race, simply because they were not prepared for a hard one. There is a big difference. I have sometimes got on a horse and been told, by the owner or trainer, not to finish in the first four because it would spoil the handicap. But in most cases, I have found, such animals would have struggled to be anywhere near the first four.

'There is no doubt that it is easy enough to get away with stopping a horse, and it sometimes needs more than sharp eyes to spot a case. If a jockey is worth his riding fee, he can get beaten easily enough. It is far harder to win than to lose!

'The film patrols which have been introduced on most courses in recent years may have reduced the instances slightly, as it would be difficult to "strangle" a really strong horse and not be picked up. But not many are that obvious. There are cases when a jockey is put in a difficult position. If he is told to stay out of the places, and the horse is pulling for his head and looking every inch a winner, what does he do? The sensible jockey will let the horse win, and save his own licence.

'Perhaps the owner hasn't had a bet. Probably he will not be too pleased. But this happens quite regularly, and if the trainer deserves any respect at all, he will support his jockey for staying out of trouble.

'Jockeys are regularly called before the local stewards under suspicion of stopping, or more frequently for alleged "schooling in public", something that I believe should be made legal. There are certain horses, big and backward animals, who can only learn from genuine race conditions. Half the time, in my view, the stewards call in a jockey only to keep the betting public satisfied that their money has been lost genuinely. But there are occasions, more often than not on the flat, when jockeys are stood down from riding for a period for alleged schooling.

'In 1966, I was to ride a horse called Dormant in the King George VI Chase on Boxing Day. He was a funny, ignorant animal, and in his previous race he was having a blow half-way round. I just sat on him for about three-quarters of a mile, then he found something extra and ran on strongly at the end. Dormant had some ability, however, and as we came into the straight in the King George, it looked as though we would finish third. But at the second last, Woodland Venture fell in front of me. I was delighted at the thought of second place—and there seemed no chance of winning with Arkle leading. But Arkle cleared the last with a broken pedal-bone and could only waddle on the flat. We came past him to win and the stewards, predictably enough, had me in—to explain the running of the previous race rather than this one. There was nothing at all crooked in it, however, and my explanation was accepted.

'I have never been stood down, but I came close to it once. I was to ride two horses at one meeting for Tim Handel. The first was a big baby, having his first run since pulling muscles and wasting in a quarter. He was not going well and not enjoying it, so I pulled him up. The other horse, quite well fancied, never got back in the race after being left six or eight lengths behind at the start.

'The stewards at the meeting did not accept the explanations of myself or the trainer and, as is the custom, we were both ordered to appear before the Jockey Club stewards at Portman Square. Tim was fined, and lost his licence for a month, but I escaped with a caution when I could very easily have been banned.

'Their case was that I had been schooling in public, but I contend it was totally innocent. The first horse was scared to gallop after his injury and the second was just not good enough. There was, however, one funny moment during the hearing when one of the senior stewards, in trying to establish my guilt, interrogated me at length about the horse with the injured leg. The only trouble was, he had become very confused and was talking about the wrong horse.

'On another occasion, I was called in for not trying hard enough on a horse, because I did not ride him out and give him a few cracks with the whip. We were just beaten for second place after I had grabbed my horse's head on the flat. But my defence was that the ground was rock hard, the horse was hating it and I saw no justification for knocking spots off him with the whip just to get second place.'

Three years ago, champion jockey John Francome's involvement with bookmaker John Banks found its way into the Jockey Club's disciplinary 'court', and inevitably onto the headlines of the sports pages. Banks received a lengthy ban from all racecourse business and Francome was suspended for six weeks. The inference was not only that Francome was tipping winners to Banks, but also that he was 'stopping' horses in collaboration with the bookmaker—an allegation he still denies.

King's view of the episode is typical of that held by most jockeys. 'What John did was illegal, but no worse, surely, than telling a friend when you think one of your rides will win. Is that so very different from a betting owner adding some cash to his jockeys' fee?'

'I do not accept that John ever lost races to orders. He simply told Banks when he fancied a horse. To outsiders, it seems to have caused a sensation, yet to those in racing it meant very little. The story was only blown up because the figures involved were so well known.'

Three years on, Francome remains unrepentant in the belief that 'my punishment was harsh'. The episode also appears to have had as much success as anything else in ruffling Francome's striking serenity. 'It didn't worry me at all. In fact, I put on two pounds in weight, which must mean I was relaxed.'

'People will always suspect the worst in a case like this, and there was very little I could do to stop them. Unfortunately, it did no good to racing, which always seems to get a bad deal by being portrayed as utterly crooked in every television programme about it.

'I have lost count of the amount of times I have been accused of stopping one, by some bloke who has sat up in the stand. The trouble is, very few people can tell the difference between a jockey actually pulling a horse, and simply holding on to his head because he is knackered and can't go any faster.

'Mr Winter, my guv'nor, knows all our horses so well that he can tell me exactly how they have run after watching me ride one from the stands. He would be the first to know if I was stopping one, and throughout the Banks business he stayed loyal and played completely fair with me. He knew that I had not thrown any races.'

Jonjo O'Neill, who has now dethroned Francome, also claims innocence in the stopping stakes. 'I can honestly say I have never stopped one in my career,' he states. 'Neither have I ever ridden for a trainer who has asked me to stop one. Even if I was asked, I would never throw away a winner. It is against everything I grew up to believe in. People in the game know that, and maybe that is why I am never asked.

'Of course, I have seen horses run badly for no apparent reason and I have thought to myself, "I could have won on that". But perhaps the fellow on top just couldn't do any better. It could just be that I am blind to this side of the game. But so long as it never interferes with what I am doing, I would prefer that it stays that way.'

There are, nevertheless, any number of jockeys willing to abide by requests to stop a horse, pervert the course of a race if you like. One particular animal I observed during the season was twice pulled so blatantly that it became a talking-point among jockeys, trainers and press. When it was finally 'off', it was beaten into second place by a short-head, having appeared from outside the betting and been backed down to favourite.

As stopping is entirely a gambling ploy, it leads neatly on to another fraught issue. Jockeys are not allowed to bet at all, either on themselves or, obviously more indicting, on other horses. Yet like everything else in sport which is branded illegal, it goes on. Generally, the punting is perfectly innocent and has no connection with crime whatever.

The stewards are still duty bound to punish offenders if and when caught, and very few jockeys are injudicious enough to place their bets themselves. There is, however, one quite unique tale of a jockey who did put on his own cash, was spotted by a steward, and still escaped. This is how he tells the story:

'I had just finished riding for the afternoon at Newbury. After changing, I fancied some jellied eels, so I walked across the course to the Silver Ring and bought some. A race was just about to start, and while I was eating my eels, I glanced at the bookies' boards. I saw what looked a very fair price on a forecast and, out of interest, I slipped a fiver on it.

'Well, it came up, and I had more than a hundred quid to collect. But just as the money was changing hands, I noticed the Racecourse Security Chief, a Brigadier, standing a few yards away watching me. I had to think quickly, and instinct told me to run. I went back across the course and out of the main gates, hailed a taxi and told the driver to take me home—about two miles from the racecourse.

'When I got there, I raced upstairs, took off all my clothes and put on a completely different set, the colours as opposite as I could get them. I even put on a hat, which I had not worn before. Then I left the house again and ran back to the racecourse. I told the fellow on the gate that he hadn't seen me and he agreed, with some persuasion. As I approached the weighing-room, the loudspeakers were calling for me to report to the stewards' room.

'Another jockey met me outside and said "I hear they've caught you punting. You'll be stood down for that". I assured him that I would not, and left him thinking about it as I composed myself and marched in. The Brigadier was sat right in front, facing me, and his face fell in complete disbelief as he looked me up and down.

'After a brief discussion, there were some muttered apologies for wasting my time, and I was released without a stain on my record. But ever since that day, whenever I see the Brigadier, he still asks me how I did it.'

Although now retired and out of racing completely, that jockey lives on in the game for that amusing story.

Jeff King's vices do not include punting, but only partly on moral grounds. 'It has never interested me to bet. I can get all the pleasure I want from a race just by watching a certain horse or jockey. Apart from that, however, it disturbs me that I have seen so many people ruin their lives by gambling away all their money. Not just those involved in racing, but working lads among my pals, who do all their wages on a single horse and lose more often than not.'

'When I left Sir Gordon Richards many years ago to join Bob Turnell's stable, I left behind a very good filly, which I had "done" as a two-year-old. She had not won a race but I knew how good she was, and when she ran for the first time the next season, in a three-year-old maiden race at Salisbury, I went to watch and put a fiver on her.

'In those days, a fiver was pretty much all I had, and I can remember literally trembling as I stood on the stand watching Scobie Breasley, riding in typical style, get her up to win by a short-head. I picked up my money, but also decided on the spot that betting was not for me. That was the last time I ever put any money on a horse.'

10 Two ways to lose

One weekend in Lancashire, and I knew what it was to lose a big race. That was my feeling on the last day of February, as King slept in the passenger seat while my right foot stayed flat on the floor and the monotony of the M6 slipped rapidly past. It was a weekend that had begun full of hope. Booked for only one ride on each of the two days at Haydock Park, King nevertheless had the satisfaction of knowing that both mounts were well-fancied, both races well rewarded. He was to ride Drusus in the Embassy Chase Final and Shaftesbury in the Victor Ludorum Hurdle, both horses for trainer Fred Rimell. Between them, the events were worth almost £25,000.

Drusus seemed likely to contest favouritism with Dramatist, trained by Fulke Walwyn and ridden by Bill Smith, and there was amusing irony in the fact that Smith was the back-seat passenger as we drove up towards Liverpool on the Friday morning. Inevitably, the big race dominated conversation. Interestingly, both jockeys spoke in a trough of pessimism about their own mount's chances. King believed that the recent rain would make the going too yielding for Drusus's liking, while Smith did not accept that Dramatist's past record justified favouritism. By the time we reached Haydock, shrouded in a damp mist yet bustling with activity, I was in a fog about just who did have any chance.

As things turned out, both King and Smith were right. Dramatist 'died' after the last fence and finished third; considerably more depressing, Drusus almost stopped as the field entered the final straight and finished last at no more than a trot. In the jockeys' vernacular, he had 'gone out like a light'.

King was philosophical. It had been too soft, he explained, and the horse's heavy fall at Nottingham two weeks earlier must have caused more damage than was known. But, as he sadly confirmed that Drusus would surely now miss both Cheltenham's Festival and the Aintree National meeting, King could have no notion of the real reason for failure.

On the way home to Rimell's yard at Kinnersely, Drusus began to cough up blood. A vet, called to examine the animal, diagnosed a blood clot on the lung, caused by the fall at Nottingham and haemorrhaged by the exertions of the Haydock race. On being told that Drusus actually completed the course, the vet was apparently astounded, and gave the opinion that any punishment from King in the final straight would undoubtedly have killed him.

All King knew that evening, however, was that his share of £16,000 had promptly vanished. There were inevitable questions from everyone he met, and few satisfactory answers. In most cases, a losing jockey is like no other sporting also-ran: a runner beaten in a sprint may know he failed to start fast enough; a batsman bowled for nought may know he played inside the line of the delivery; a footballer missing a penalty may know he struck the shot too wide. A beaten jockey can only wonder why his horse did not run to form.

We stayed half-an-hour from the course that night, with a marvellously hospitable horse-owner and his wife. Neither of them had ever met King or I until that day, but the introduction, effected by trainer 'Ginger' McCain, was enough. We were fed and watered lavishly and then, around midnight, we walked half a mile to inspect the man's horses.

At 2.30 a.m. I was still playing in the house's snooker room, but five hours later I was on Southport beach, having the cobwebs blown out of my system as I watched McCain's horses work on the sand. It was the best method I've ever discovered for curing a hangover.

Mugs of tea in the kitchen of 'Ginger's' Southport home were complemented by an introduction to an animal who, even to my untutored eyes, possessed the unmistakeable intelligence of a sporting genius. The incomparable Red Rum was peering out of his box—the end one, closest to the house—with an alert curiosity. An hour earlier, when the horses still in training had moved off for their exercise, 'Rummy' had, as always, stamped his feet and complained, disgruntled that his racing days were past.

King breakfasted on toast and tea, declining the offer of an expansive grill, then soaked in the bath and contemplated the task facing Shaftesbury. A daunting one certainly, in this high-class hurdle race for four-year-olds, but his own confidence in the horse's potential had been supported by the news, in that morning's racing press, that a substantial four-figure bet had been placed on Shaftesbury to win the Triumph Hurdle at Cheltenham.

As so often, he had to deal diplomatically with those pestering for tips, badgering him to say his horse would win. He had a chance, he declared—and would venture no further.

It was a slowly-run race, against King's wishes, and although he crossed the second last in the leading pack with every chance, a little bumping and boring ruled out the small and lightly-built Shaftesbury from even the minor places.

King was subdued and thoughtful, the closest I saw him to being truly upset. It was a lost weekend, financially worth nothing more than three riding fees—he had picked up a spare on the Saturday—less food and petrol, and worth a minus amount in terms of morale and future planning. A winning jockey can generally count on retaining the successful horse as a regular ride for a time. A loser has no such peace of mind.

The evening did nothing to improve Jeff's spirits. It should have been a sociable night—Lorna Vincent's 21st birthday party under the racecourse stand at Newbury—but King survived only half an hour before having to retire to his car and sleep off the after-effects of fatigue and the growing effects of a stomach bug.

While Jeff King spent the afternoon of March 4 riding one obscure horse in an obscure race at Warwick, the racing fraternity and a million monarchy-minded housewives directed their attentions south to Sussex, and the Plumpton course on which the heir to the throne was making his race-riding debut.

Although deep in jump-racing time, this was a flat event, totally for charity and restricted to amateurs. A number of celebrities were involved but they might as well have stayed at home. HRH Prince Charles achieved a monopoly of interest.

His horse, Long Wharf, was the subject of so much betting, albeit mainly flutters of the ten pence to ten bob variety, that it started a very warm favourite. Despite being given a competent ride, however, he was beaten into second place by BBC sports commentator Derek Thompson.

The sun shone, the close ring of bodyguards surrounding the Prince was superfluous and everyone went home happy. The day had just one minor incident which merited a mention in few of the papers. Believing themselves to be thoughtful to a prospective King who was unlikely to relish mixing with a few dozen earthy jockeys, the executive of Plumpton provided a fitted caravan for the Prince to change in. They were no doubt surprised to find their star guest rebuking them for such élitist views and insisting on using the general weighing-room.

Four days later, to the fanfare of even greater interest and specially extended television racing coverage, the Prince made his first attempt at steeplechasing in the Military meeting at Sandown Park. His appearance put a thousand or so on the course attendance, created heaven knows how many racing converts via the television, and ended in a modest triumph with the Prince finishing the course, but in a remote last place, on an honest, plodding horse called Sea Swell, whose trainer Nick Gaselee had one other runner at the meeting—Doddington Park, ridden by Jeff King.

Inside the Sandown weighing-room, the amateurs involved in the Prince's race were grouped into a corner. Some of the pros were apprehensive of approaching their heir but valet John Buckingham reports that Jeff had no such inhibitions and was first to go up and talk racing. 'I found him tremendous,' says King. 'He was quite happy to mix and chat—in fact he hated the thought of being treated any differently.'

Richard Evans was one of those who struggled to overcome a certain shyness—'I eventually went up and wished him luck very quickly', he recalls—but he does provide a mischievously amusing tale about him.

'A week or so before the Prince's first ride, Nick Gaselee asked me to ride out for him one morning. I drove down from Stratford very early, and we were all ready to pull out of his yard in Lambourn on time at 7.30 a.m. The minutes ticked by and at twenty-to-eight I asked one of the lads what we were waiting for. The answer was Prince Charles.'

The Prince, apparently, duly arrived and was to ride Sea Swell. But as the rest moved off, the royal rider remained in the yard, his mount declining to move one inch. For some strange reason, Sea Swell had decided he was not going to budge, Prince or no Prince, and needed a great deal of persuasion to change his mind.

11 Cheltenham

It might seem irreverent to laugh, but quite the most amusing sight of the 1980 Cheltenham Festival occurred in the drizzle of the opening afternoon, as an over-excited Irish priest celebrated a winner. Clad in the sober black robes of his vocation, dog-collar showing beneath a vast grin, he leaped high in the air as the Irish-trained Anaglogs Daughter passed the post to win the Arkle Chase. Yelping emotionally, he then slapped both palms of his friend's hands in the style of West Indian cricketers after taking a wicket, then bolted past me like an Olympic sprinter and was lost from sight, presumably to claim his dues from the bookie.

The star of this particular story would by no means have felt lonely or conspicuous. The holy men from across the Irish Sea appeared everywhere throughout the three-day meeting, and the suspicion that the country's confession-boxes must have remained unmanned for the duration of the Festival coincided with the certainty that they would be dealing with queues in the week that followed.

Englishmen may like a bet, but they are non-runners when confronted with the Irish. They invade with bulging wallets for this highlight of the jumping season, seemingly intent on a non-stop orgy of gambling and guzzling to be concluded only when the last bar closes or the last pound is spent, whichever comes the sooner.

They back their home-bred horses with loyal and unequivocal passion, and the Irishman who is content with the housewives' choice, 50-pence each-way flutter, is indeed a rarity. The Tote, whose customary concession to big-spenders on English courses is the £5 windows of their betting shops, instal a number of £50 windows at Cheltenham, and they are far from unpopular. The individual bookies, meanwhile, find themselves dealing in hundreds far more often than usual—while the more serious Irish punters invest thousands. Perhaps the best-known, J. P. McManus, also the owner of a number of useful horses, admitted on television just before the Festival began that he has more than once stood to win a quarter of a million pounds on a single race.

To the English, generally speaking, a bet adds interest to an afternoon at the races. To the Irish at Cheltenham, the racing adds interest to the betting.

The jockeys take in all this with an amused tolerance, and get on with the job of riding at the most prestigious and influential meeting of the year. The Grand National may be the most famous steeplechase in the world, but the Cheltenham meeting provides three days of unbroken, top-class races. To ride a good winner or two there is to guarantee yourself valuable publicity and, almost inevitably, the offer of better rides in the immediate future.

To an Irishman like Jonjo O'Neill, the meeting perhaps holds even greater significance. He was brought up on the legends of Cheltenham and came to England with half-baked dreams he never imagined he could exceed.

'Where I come from, Cheltenham is a constant talking point,' he says. 'It is the place to go in racing. The Irish interest in the meeting is fanatical—the punters may get carried away with their gambling, but it is an obsession with the owners and trainers, too. They want a winner at Cheltenham, and for many, the entire season is aimed at that objective.

'When I was young, I watched Tommy Carberry, Pat Taafe and the other Irish greats ride at the meeting, on television. I used to hope that, one day, I might get to the course and watch it for myself. I never dared to believe I might ride there.

'My first time at the Festival was 1972. I was apprenticed to Gordon Richards, and I stayed overnight before the Gold Cup, then led up our horse, Titus Oates, for Ron Barry to ride. We've stayed close since those days, Ron and I, and it seems strange to look back on it now that we are both riding at the Festival.

'It was later that same year that I got my first ride over the Cheltenham course ... not in the Festival, but one of the big autumn races, the Mackeson Gold Cup. I had had only three previous rides over fences, and it was a bit of a break for me to get one in such a race.'

With unforgiving honesty, Jonjo completes the story, chuckling: 'I had every chance of winning as I came to the last on Proud Stone, upsides Jimmy Fox on Red Candle. I went for a big one, but jumped myself clean out of the saddle. I was on my backside, feeling pretty foolish, as Red Candle passed the post.'

O'Neill, however, arrived at the 1980 Festival as Britain's number one jockey, close to 100 winners for the season and with his second Jockey Championship more of a formality than he would ever admit. Fox arrived as Toby Balding's assistant trainer, depressed and disillusioned with the rules which still forbade him his comeback as a jockey.

For Jeff King, Cheltenham still held the appeal, if not the promise. Approaching the close of one of his leanest seasons, he had no expectations of a winner at the Festival. Of his four mounts spread over the three days, only Shaftesbury, in the *Daily Express* Triumph Hurdle, was prominent at any stage, and the mud ensured even that challenge was fruitless.

In effect, despite all the attendant glamour, charisma and publicity, it was just another meeting for King. There were no special preparations, no special plans. The week leading up to Cheltenham, in fact, had been as good an example of a normal week as one might find.

Monday's racing had been at Windsor, Tuesday at Warwick, Wednesday Worcester, Thursday Wincanton and Friday and Saturday, Sandown Park. Clocking the daily mileage from his Wiltshire home, King drove slightly more than 1,000 miles in the six days, paying, of course, all his own petrol and sundry expenses. He had only one ride each day, apart from at Worcester, where he rode two. None of his seven mounts were winners, and only one, Doddington Park in Sandown's Saturday meeting, finished in the frame. His riding fees for the week, at £32 per horse, amounted to £224.

If his personal gains from Cheltenham week were minimal, however, King took visible pleasure from the fortune bestowed on others. When his close friend and near neighbour, Steve Knight, won his second race of the Festival on 9 to 1 shot Prince of Bermuda, King was smiling as if he had won the race himself. 'That,' he declared, 'will do Steve a hell of a lot of good. Trainers take notice of riders who win at this meeting. You can bet he will pick up more rides from now on.'

King admits he is fortunate. 'I can get all the interest and excitement I need from a race just by watching one horse, or one jockey,' he says. 'I know not many are like me—many jockeys don't enjoy watching when they are uninvolved, and many racegoers have no interest unless they have their money on something. I've never needed that, which is just as well with so much time on my hands in a three-day meeting like this.'

Steve Smith-Eccles, prowling around Cheltenham like a caged tiger, provided King's antithesis. Out of action for the third time since Christmas, on this occasion with a broken collarbone, injuries had cost Steve all interest in the Jockeys' Championship and now even threatened his Grand National ride on the clear favourite, Zongalero. He was talkative and outwardly lively as ever. But predominantly, he was bored.

'I don't usually come to racing if I'm not riding,' he explained. 'I don't enjoy watching unless I'm involved, and I don't think I've ever been so bored as I am here.' He stuck out his chin in the familiar pose which reflects his determination, and added: 'It's sociable enough, and I'm all for the odd night out with a few whiskies. But this can't compare with being out there, in the middle of the action.'

He was present every day, though, wandering, a little forlorn, a little envious, into the unsaddling enclosure where the cheering and jubilation which greets each winning horse and rider is like nothing I'd seen on a

John Burke, who tasted the extremes of success and depression so early in his career, back in action in 1980.

The many faces of the race-going public.

TOP: Jim Wilson is the only rider not caked in mud, having led from the off on Willie Wumpkins in the 1980 Cheltenham Festival. Rest of the front rank are (left to right) John Francome, Jonjo O'Neill, Ted Waite and Lorna Vincent.

ABOVE: The eyes of both horse and rider bulge in excitement ... Stopped and Ben de Haan, winning at Cheltenham, 1980.

racecourse before. And, like the rest of us, Steve witnessed more striking examples of the perennial habit this steeplechasing game has of setting up its heroes, and then knocking them down.

Tommy Carberry and Dessie Hughes, two of Ireland's most distinguished and successful riders, were two who tasted triumph and pain within a matter of hours, or, in Carberry's case, even less.

Displaying the skills of a sensitive, intelligent rider, Carberry urged his mount Tied Cottage through the mud to claim his fourth Cheltenham Gold Cup, equalling the record held by Pat Taafe. The Irish were rightly ecstatic, Carberry a deserving idol. He was lifted off his feet by delighted friends and fellow jockeys, and chaired back into the weighing-room. Less than an hour later, he was in hospital after a crashing fall from the favourite, Mighty's Honour, in the next race. A broken arm was suspected, though later ruled out, but Carberry's celebrations were promptly cut short and his remaining rides given up.

Hughes was even unluckier. His Festival began with shattering disappointment, ended in shattering agony. In the Champion Hurdle, highlight of the opening day, Hughes was the partner of Monksfield, a horse little bigger than a pit pony yet backed down to 6 to 5 to win for the third consecutive year. The Irish contingent roared in confident expectation as Monksfield took up the running on the home turn, but were silenced by the English as Sea Pigeon, his old adversary, stormed through under the guidance of O'Neill, to win by seven lengths.

His pride barely restored by victory on Chinrullah in the Queen Mother's Champion Chase on the second day, Hughes then rode Light the Wad in the three-mile Sun Alliance Chase. He fell, broke his left arm and needed only hours to announce his retirement from race-riding to start a new career as a trainer.

Smith-Eccles saw all this, and saw too the change in his good friend John Burke, another Irishman with a story to tell. When the two of them went out for the evening in Cheltenham on the first night of the meeting, Burke—once a man who loved a drink—supped nothing stronger than orange juice and soda water. He had, he explained, been to the extremes of success and failure in this life. He did not intend to waste his second chance ...

In 1976, John Burke won the Cheltenham Gold Cup and the Grand National. Most jockeys dream of winning one or the other; Burke completed the double in a single season. In steeplechase racing, you can achieve little more than that ... which was Burke's problem. In slightly more than two years, he was gone. His will to work had vanished and he returned to Ireland, where he stayed until he felt ready to ride again.

'I came to Fred Rimell's yard eight years ago,' Burke related, 'and spent almost three seasons riding as an amateur, just as I had done in Ireland. When I turned pro, I started riding winners before I knew where I was.

'It was a big thing, you know. I'd grown up in County Meath, the son of a schoolteacher but in an area where racing is a bug and Cheltenham is the mecca, and now here I was, being successful in England.

'It was such a fantastic start that I let it affect me in entirely the wrong way. When I won the Gold Cup and the National, I subconsciously believed that everything was too easy. Success had come too early, I suppose. Mentally, I was not capable of handling it all and I went off the rails.

'Racing is the greatest of levellers. You look back through the formbook and see how many jockeys have ridden big winners and then disappeared into obscurity. Well, that happened to me—but I was lucky. There aren't too many who get a second bite at this level.'

Burke makes no excuses about his demise. He was totally honest as he pointed to the grey, rain-filled sky above Cheltenham for emphasis. 'One month, I was up there in the clouds and could do no wrong. The next, I was a nobody—and by the time I realised, it was too late.'

'Fred Rimell probably saved my career. He could have sounded off to someone about it, and it would have been in the papers then. That would have been it—the end. Instead, he took it all and let me slip away almost unnoticed. I was terrible, I didn't turn up for work unless I felt like it, I had no desire to ride out, no real enthusiasm left for race-riding.

'It sounds dreadful when I look back, but the fact was I did nothing for three months when I went back to Ireland. Nothing at all. I had made enough money from racing to get by, so for a while I didn't worry.

'Gradually, though, I began to get the nagging urge to ride again. I started by riding out at home, and I enjoyed it so much that I made up my mind I had to get back. Again, Mr Rimell has been good to me. He has taken me back, given me rides and kept faith. Not many would have done that for someone who let them down.

'In many ways, I am more enthusiastic about racing now than I have ever been. I go out with a positive attitude. I'm not blinkered any more, I know success is not cheap and I've got to work. But I've got my aims and ambitions mapped out now. I want to go on riding for a bit, getting as many winners as I can, paying a few people back, and then I'd like to train.

'I have always got on well with most of the lads, and I know there are a lot who are delighted to see me back. But I shan't slip back into the old ways.'

In his gentle Irish brogue, his short hair cropped over a mischievous face, Burke was talking like a contented man. He gestured at the winners' enclosure in front of us and recalled: 'Coming in there after winning the Gold Cup on Royal Frolic was the greatest moment of my riding life. It beat winning the National, you know. The Gold Cup is the

Blue Riband race, the one every jockey wants ... but then, to win any race at this meeting gives you an incredible feeling. Mind, you need a hell of a horse to win—so many 'run out of petrol' as they come round that final bend and up the hill. But for those who make it, the walk back in here, and the roar of that crowd is a fantastic experience.'

John Burke did not win a race at Cheltenham this year. In truth, he did not really come close. But he rode, he took part, he was back. And very glad just to be there.

Ben de Haan and Apprenticeship

Those who watched the jockey rather than the horse as Stopped won the last race of the first-day card at Cheltenham, might have noticed a wide, disbelieving grin on the face of Ben de Haan. And those who knew him would have understood.

Only 42 days earlier, Ben had still been impatiently awaiting the first winner of his young career. Now here he was, with the full-blown roar of the Cheltenham masses in his ears, winning with his first-ever mount at the Festival meeting.

The big, round eyes of this 20-year-old were bulging with emotion as he dismounted before the crowd around the winners' enclosure, accepted the backslaps and congratulations and made his way back to the weighing-room. He had ridden with professional tidiness and composure, achieved the first major break of his racing life, and was now in something of a daze.

But if he needed something to bring him down to earth, Ben did not have long to wait. He returned that evening to Lambourn, to Fred Winter's yard where he had worked for almost five years, to the long, wooden shack which was home to him and 14 other lads, and to the tiny box room with two bunks and precious little else which he shared with another aspiring young rider.

The champagne and caviar had to wait a few years. Ben had a quiet drink at the course, reflected on the day over a coffee at the hostel, and retired to his bunk. After all, he had to be up, as usual, at 6.30 a.m.

De Haan is just one of the legion of stable-lads to whom a race-ride is a glittering highspot and a winner a dream in an existence which combines unsocial hours with mucky, repetitive work and a fair share of drudgery. Most top jockeys made their way in the sport through this route or the flat-racing apprenticeship and, if few can honestly claim to have enjoyed every part of it, they at least have the knowledge that they have made it the hard way.

A sizeable proportion, of course, do not make it at all, and if success in the saddle is elusive they have two options—to make a career of being a stable-lad, or to quit the racing game altogether. De Haan seems unlikely to be forced into such a decision now—but for some years, as frustration gnawed away at his ambitions, the future looked like developing into anything but a Cheltenham festival winner at the first attempt.

'I had been here four years before I had my first ride,' he recalled. 'There were many occasions during that time when I thought I was in the wrong job. If I hadn't got a licence and started riding this season, I don't know whether I would still be here.'

The morning after his Cheltenham win, I joined Ben for breakfast. It was nine o'clock and I still felt heavy-lidded and bleary, but the pitch of conversation in the small, cramped room which serves as the hostel's dining area reminded me that these lads had been up and working for several hours.

Hot, strong tea was poured from a giant, old-fashioned pot, sliced bread and butter waited in a mini-mountain on the serving hatch, behind which the hostel chef cooked sausages and bacon while Terry Wogan's cheery banter blared from a portable radio. A few easy chairs at one end of the room were occupied and the conversation was dominated by racing. Ben himself bore the brunt of inevitable, good-natured ribbing for the attentions his winner had earned.

We adjourned to Ben's room to talk and he uncovered a chair, hidden by the curtains, for me to sit on. One side of the room was occupied by two bunks, the other by shelves for clothes and a few personal belongings. In between, there was just about room for three people to stand. 'It's hardly luxury,' agreed Ben. 'But until this year, we had to get four lads in rooms little bigger than this.'

The de Haans, a name of Dutch origin although all Ben's recent ancestors have been Londoners, are not a racing family. Ben, however, developed an interest in horses at the pony-riding stage, graduated to show-jumping and hunting and, refusing to be discouraged by the warnings that he was too tall, made up his mind that he would be a jockey.

'It all started when I was five or six, and my mother was housekeeper to a trainer, Charlie Smith. My interest grew from those days, and eventually it was Charlie who had a word with Mr Winter and got me a job here.

'I was just 16 when I started, and my wage was £2 a week. Our Association was formed pretty soon afterwards, so I was lucky—I was quickly earning £10 a week. Our board and food is free, though, and nobody complains.'

Ben lit a cigarette from a packet of ten, took a gulp of tea and went on to describe the average day in a stable-lad's life.

'We have to be up around 6.30 a.m. I normally wake unaided, but anyone who oversleeps will soon hear the head lad shouting outside his door. There is no time to do anything but wash and dress, then we're outside, mucking out our own horses. Until a few weeks ago, I had three to do. Now that I'm race-riding more regularly, I just have two—Rough and Tumble, our Grand National entry, and Stopped ... I didn't mind mucking him out today!

'We tack up at 7.30 a.m., and we move off with the first lot at 7.45 a.m. On Mondays, we take them on the roads, Tuesdays, Thursdays and Saturdays it's usually up on the downs. Wednesday is an easy day—just some gentle exercise. By nine, we are back in the yard for breakfast—a half-hour break. Then the head lad is round to shout us out again, this time to sweep the yards, or in my case tidy the tack rooms. About an hour later, we take out the second lot of horses for exercise.

'After that, it's time to clean your bridles, tidy everything up in your own boxes, and then feed. Everyone is responsible for feeding their own horses, so there might be a bit of a rush to get into the feed room first. At about 12.15 p.m. we are finished until four o'clock.

'I never do a lot with that break. I might clean my car, play pool in the common room, or walk down into Lambourn village to buy a snack for lunch.

'When it is time to restart, we dress the horses over and muck out the boxes again. Then we sweep the yards once more before the guv'nor's evening inspection at 5.30 p.m. Six o'clock is evening feed, another race to be first, and we are free from about half-past.

'Every other week, we get Saturday afternoon and Sunday off. I go home to see my parents in Maidenhead then. But in the course of each fortnight, we work $12\frac{1}{2}$ days ... there can't be many jobs left in which that happens.

'Our evenings are quiet, generally. I don't go out in Lambourn much because I don't think it's worth it. I hardly drink at all now, although I will have one or two bacardis when I go home to take out my girlfriend, every Wednesday night.'

There are no special concessions to the lads who have rides on a racing day. 'I often miss breakfast to get everything done,' said Ben, 'and if racing is not too far away, say Newbury or one of the London courses, I have to get back in time for evening stables. We're not allowed to hang around drinking and socialising with the older jockeys.'

Brian Delaney, the experienced head lad, was testing his vocal chords outside Ben's window now. It was time to return. Breakfast was over. But before he left, Ben recalled the greatest day so far in his racing life.

'I thought I had got past the stage of being nervous before a race, but I admit I was jittery yesterday. I don't have any superstitions, but I just changed quietly, not saying much to anyone. I was surprised by the atmosphere in the weighing-room—I thought there might be a lot of tension, it being Cheltenham, but there was plenty of laughing and joking as usual.

'The nerves disappeared when I got out to the paddock. I felt fine then. I expected the guv'nor to give me some instructions, but in fact he said I knew how to ride Stopped better than he did. Brian Delaney said more, though. He's been here a long time, knows his job and all the horses. He told me I should be handy behind the leaders at the top of the hill, then let him bolt down it.

'It didn't quite work out to plan, because he bolted so fast that we were much farther ahead than I'd wanted to be. But he was going so well that I just let him run.

'I talk to this horse as we're going round—a lot of nonsense really but maybe it helps me concentrate. He pulls a lot, and for most of the time I'm just calling him names. He gave me a tremendous ride yesterday, though.

'I know I was grinning when we passed the post. I was thinking to myself that I used to hate the horse because he scraped up his bed, sweated up a lot and was generally a bloody nuisance to look after. I only ride him because John Francome doesn't like him—but I'm not complaining now.

'It hasn't sunk in yet. Maybe it won't for a day or two. But coming back to this, to the hard work and the hostel, must keep my feet on the ground. I suppose it would be hard for someone like John to come back to this kind of work after winning at Cheltenham, but I think it's made it easier for me. I've floated through today.'

Ben de Haan pulled his boots back on, squeezed out of the door and went back to work in the damp morning mist ... the successful apprentice of modern times. Rather more than 20 years earlier, and just down the road in Marlborough, Jeff King had set out on a very similar life, in a remarkably similar way.

'I was with Sir Gordon Richards from the age of 15 to 18$^{1}/_{2}$,' he recalls. 'It was the usual thing that got me in; I belonged to a Pony Club, someone knew I was keen to get into racing and recommended me to Sir Gordon ... and not much has changed in the life of a lad or an apprentice since then.

'We started at 7 a.m., worked until 12.30 p.m. and then took a break until four. We finished at 6.30 p.m. and had the evenings free. The real difference is that our only time off was every third Sunday afternoon. Other than that, we worked seven days a week and thought no more about it.

'I only ever looked after two horses. People wanted to work in those days, there were more lads about, less horses to go round. I got heavy quite quickly and knew I would never make a flat jockey, so I just waited and waited for my first ride over jumps. There was no question of pushing, or asking the guv'nor. You just waited until you were asked.

'When I started out, we got paid ten shillings a week. On top of that, of course, we were fed and clothed. We lived in a long, barrack-type hostel and all slept in one room, like a dormitory. There were 12 or 15 of us most of the time, and only one bath, one shower and a couple of basins to go round.

'But I think lads were happier in those days, perhaps because there were not so many choices of careers, not so much leisure time and social distractions. All we knew was that we could have a bloody good night out for less than three bob. The cinema in Marlborough was our favourite. Our fare, there and back on the bus, cost about sixpence, it was a shilling to get into the pictures, and we could buy a packet of fags for sevenpence and a couple of halves of beer on the way home for about the same. When we didn't go out in the evenings, there was a snooker table and a television in the hostel.

'My aunt and uncle, Peg and Reg, used to drive down to take me out on my Sunday off. When we got back to the yard, later the same evening, Peg would usually start crying. She thought it was awful that I had to live in such conditions. But she was just being soft. It may not have been luxury, but I never worried about it. It was just like being in the army, really.'

On the last afternoon of the Cheltenham Festival, King watched from the stand as Ben de Haan, a generation beneath him, attempted a momentous double. 'Stopped' was running again, in the final race of the card, and had been backed down to a short-priced favourite.

Climbing the hilly back straight, Stopped was three lengths clear and cruising. But one blunder put paid to the dream. Horse and rider clattered into the wet, slushy turf. Ben rose unharmed, but was left with the time it takes to walk ingloriously across the Cheltenham track to mull it all over. The great leveller was at work again. Today, Ben was just a lad who fell.

12 The Grand National

Champagne bottles littered the lawns and terraces like some crazy attempt at decoration. Betting tickets, disgustedly discarded, mingled with squashed paper cups and *The Sporting Lifes*—race-cards would have joined them but the printers had chosen Grand National day to strike.

It was six in the evening on March 29 and the sun was still shining gently on Aintree racecourse. The first rush of departures was over, and those who were left seemed content to wind down slowly as the evening drifted by.

Inside the weighing-room, relative calm had returned after the chaos of the perennial greatest day in the steeplechasing calendar. The valets counted their tack, their tips and their headaches in the two adjoining rooms, now unguarded yet earlier protected fiercely by a handful of Aintree's garrison of gatemen.

Only a few jockeys remained of the 30 who had started out for the National and the dozens more who were there for other rides—or just for the ride. Champion John Francome, whose composure had never shown the slightest sign of disturbance throughout the day, chatted happily about Rough and Tumble, the horse on which he had finished third last year and second this; chatted too, about his personal bid to gain more sponsorship freedom for jockeys—he had worn his initials down the legs of his breeches for the National.

Andy Turnell left with Francome, forcing a weak smile through the winces of his limp, occasioned by falling at the third fence. And then only one rider remained, deep in the corner of the weighing-room, sitting disconsolately with his head lad and covering once more the hopeless story of his lost afternoon. This was Brod Munro-Wilson, city gent, target for sneers and cynics yet a braver and bolder individualist than many who snipe at him. He had genuinely believed he could win, become the first amateur to own and train his own horse and triumph this century. He had been beaten by a freak of science before having the chance to find out if he and his mount were good enough.

As the sun went down that night on Liverpool racecourse and its frightening fences, as the clearing-up began, the inquests continued and the traffic jams eased, the place reverted to its hibernation state for another 363 days; until March 1981, when the final Thursday of the month would again bring with it that very special feeling. Cheltenham and its Festival may have the best cards and provide the better tests of consistent skill. But Aintree and its National will remain the dream-maker. And the heartbreaker.

The three-day meeting in 1980 apparently attracted 90,000 customers through the gates. Of that figure, 70,000 were present on National day, straining their eyes from every fence and every bank of grass quite apart from the more orthodox and expensive terraces and stands.

But the atmosphere, every jockey will tell you, is present from Thursday onwards. There is a sense of impending occasion, of rising tension. There is also an awareness and acceptance of the dangers involved, and perhaps it is this which explains why the customary cameraderie of the breed is accentuated at Liverpool.

Most jockeys stay at Liverpool for the duration of the meeting, but some prefer to put up with the hours of travelling in order to get home each night. Francome has often completed the 400-mile round trip from Liverpool to Lambourn on each day of the National meeting; Richard Evans prefers driving back to Stratford-on-Avon each evening. Those who do stay up tend to cling to favourite hotels. Liverpool's Holiday Inn is popular, particularly with the younger jockeys; amateur Munro-Wilson chose the exclusive Adelphi. But a long-time loyalty exists between a number of riders and an expansive old hotel on Southport promenade, once called the Royal but now combined to become the Royal Clifton.

It is a charming cross between a seaside hotel and a colonial-style resting place. High ceilings, large rooms, long corridors and creaking stairs contribute to an atmosphere which persuades many to stay faithful despite the attractions and amenities of more modern hotels. In National week, it is always fully booked, and those not going to the races are cast in the same mould as foreigners. Its atmosphere also breeds a sense of fun which is never far from the average jump jockey.

On the evening that we arrived, Jeff King had just phoned the reception desk to complain that his automatic teasmade was not working. Royal jockey Bill Smith was checking in at the time, and beckoned to the telephonist to put him on the line. Smith then adopted a high-pitched bleat and impersonated a gay maintenance man who 'would love to come and put you right, Mr King.' The phone was slammed down and Jeff prepared to repel invaders until someone told him the identity of his caller.

Socially, jump jockeys are rarely inhibited. At Liverpool, most will enjoy eating out and many will drink to their usual intake limit. Others, mindful of their weight or simply of the occasion, restrict themselves to a plain meal and an early night.

For the peripheral people, however, the National meeting is

something of a binge. Betting by day and boozing by night would not be an inaccurate description of the week for many individuals, and hotel bar parties, begun in small and quiet groups, gather unplanned into a noisy celebration which can continue through to breakfast.

Not for everyone is the National a comfortable break. Ben de Haan, for instance, was an instant celebrity when winning on Stopped at Cheltenham. Now he was back in the guise of travelling stable-lad, 'doing' Fred Winter's Rough and Tumble, just as he had for most of his apprenticeship. No luxury hotels for de Haan and fellow lads—just the old converted hospital attached to the Aintree stables which serves as a hostel.

'It is pretty desperate,' reported Ben. 'It doesn't matter what time of night you get to bed, you're not going to sleep well. The sleeping quarters have wooden floorboards on which you can hear a pin drop—let alone a group of lads blundering back from a few drinks.'

De Haan arrived with his charge on Friday afternoon and smilingly admitted that he could scarcely wait for the year when he might himself ride in the National. But there were two jockeys that day who believed that they had only 24 hours to wait ... but were proved wrong.

Irishman Tommy Carberry started the day with a lot in his favour. Just a fortnight earlier, he had won the Gold Cup on Tied Cottage. Now, he was to ride Seventh Son, favourite for the Sean Graham Trophy Chase, as a potentially lucrative pipe-opener for his National ride on Delmoss.

A few hours later, everything had gone horribly wrong. Just before leaving the weighing-room to ride Seventh Son, Carberry was told that a routine dope test on Tied Cottage had proved positive and he would almost inevitably lose the race. Still reeling from such sensational news, his whole week literally fell apart when Seventh Son fell at the second fence. Carberry took a fierce kick in the head and was unconscious for some time. He came round on the way to hospital but was concussed and had broken his collar-bone. In the space of less than an hour, he had lost victory in the Gold Cup and any chance of winning the Grand National.

The plight of young English jockey Bryan Smart made no such headlines yet was equally distressing. He had been engaged to ride Churchtown Boy, a long shot but, at 13, the oldest horse in the race and one seasoned with Aintree experience. But with one day left, he was summarily told that the horse's owners had decided Andy Turnell should have the ride. Smart was inconsolable, and understandably so. It was rather like giving a child a marvellous birthday present, then taking it back and giving it to another.

Jeff King said: 'I feel terribly sorry for him, but the longer you are in racing, the less you can be surprised by such things. Loyalty is not one of this sport's most obvious qualities.'

No-one blamed Turnell, and by the end of the day, most were sympathising after the stewards had referred him to the Jockey Club for 'sentence' on a charge of excessive use of the whip. Apart from financial gain, the ride on Churchtown Boy did little to raise his spirits, as he was among the earliest fallers.

Rain fell in torrents for much of Friday afternoon, and was so heavy during the second race that Jonjo O'Neill had to pull up his fancied mount because, he explained, he could not see a thing. By the end of racing, however, the sun was pushing through the clouds and another of the traditions—the walk of the course—went ahead as planned.

Several jockeys accompany the public on a guided tour of the National fences. Among them was Richard Linley, due to ride So and So in the big race. 'I might as well scare myself to sleep tonight,' was his wry comment as he set off.

I postponed my own view of the fences until Saturday morning, which dawned cold, grey but dry. Breakfast was a remarkably vibrant meal, considering the excesses of many just a few hours earlier, and conversation around the tables with their spattered white covers scarcely veered from the topic of the day.

Outside, the hotel's car park was littered with confetti, a relic of a Friday night wedding reception but a reminder of a comment passed by Steve Smith-Eccles, rider of the ante-post favourite Zongalero, who had finished second last year. 'He's always been a bit of a bridesmaid,' he had told me. 'But he's going to get married on Saturday!'

In the newsagents round the corner, a black cat sat morosely atop a pile of children's comics, as if waiting to spring in front of a lucky jockey. The wind was blowing off the sea in freezing gusts, rattling the morning papers in the stand outside the shop. Every paper had its National supplement. Every paper picked its winner with brash confidence. Every paper was wrong.

It was just after 11 a.m. when I arrived at the course, but the place was bustling. Out on the course, hundreds of curious punters, wrapped up in several layers of clothing against the weather, examined each fence with gasps and grunts.

Policehorses and guards with alsatians patrolled quietly while this morning ritual ran its course. Some eternal optimists were battling to set up their picnic on the bank overlooking the third fence, the awesome one fronted by a ditch and with a six-foot drop on the landing side. Further along the track, past the legendary Bechers and the relatively tame next fence—now famous for the pile-up which allowed Foinavon through at 100 to 1 in 1967—a group of bookies were stationing themselves by The Canal Turn, that dramatic fence at which the field are forced to turn 90 degrees to their left on landing. The music piping from the speakers on that remote and bleak corner of the course was the theme to the television series *All Creatures Great and Small*, all about the lives of a company of vets. How fitting.

The first race was at 2.0 p.m. and by then the atmosphere was taut. The tops of the stands had filled, the queues for the Tote bookies were lengthening by the minute as hundreds of housewives' fifty-pences were ploughed on horses with nice names and thousands of pounds were invested on horses supposed to have every credential for the course and the going. In the National, however, a bet is a gamble in every sense of the word, and this year's race was to be the clearest proof of that.

Television cameras were camped in their usual corner of the winners' enclosure, and as the build-up to the race continued, David Coleman, smiling and superbly professional, interviewed a selection of the jockeys. Some looked more nervous about that than the race.

Twenty-five minutes before the scheduled off, the riders filed out of the weighing-room and made their way to the parade-ring, by now the centre of attraction. Jenny Hembrow, the only lady jockey, was fittingly first out; Steve Smith-Eccles followed, chewing intently and looking grim. Jonjo O'Neill was grinning as ever, John Francome was coolly chatty as ever, Linley looked tense, Turnell worried. Phil Blacker, having won the preceding race on Pollardstown, looked deservedly self-satisfied and continued to do so all afternoon. Somewhere in the line, but unrecognised by me at least, was the American amateur Charlie Fenwick, vigorously rotating the ever-present gum around his mouth at the start of a race he would never forget.

The tiny parade-ring resembled Waterloo Station on a Friday evening as the announcement for jockeys to mount was made. Then, just as suddenly, it was empty. Horses and jockeys were en route for the course, owners and trainers treading carefully through the mud to their private stand, the public scattering rapidly from the viewing bank and sprinting to obtain some sort of position. Many would see nothing more of the race than the flash of colours as the field passed the stand for the first time, and a glimpse of the lonely winner about five minutes later.

In all, the race occupied ten minutes and seventeen seconds. Not long, really, for the most dramatic and compulsive viewing of any British sporting occasion. After all the build-up, all the tension and speculation, the race seemed over almost before it had begun.

Not, however, for Charlie Fenwick. The merchant banker from Baltimore enjoyed the experience of his life as challengers dropped off with alarming regularity and left him, and his mount Ben Nevis, many lengths clear as he rounded the final turn into the straight.

Even as the massed crowd in the stands loomed into his view, and with it the winning-post, John Francome was putting in a despairing final effort to foil Fenwick. But despairing it was, Ben Nevis drew on reserves of strength and energy and passed the post looking fit for another circuit. Fenwick's face had split into a cavernous grin at the triumphant fulfilment of what for him had nothing to do with livelihood or future career. It was simply an amateur's adventure.

Just what went through Fenwick's mind as he returned to the unsaddling enclosure, even he could not say. Words are never easily found at such moments of achievement, and even the eloquent American was reduced to trite platitudes. His smile, however, wrote a book for him.

Greeted by the traditional cheer from the crowd surrounding the enclosure, Fenwick dismounted and was almost instantly grabbed by two policemen, one on each arm, and frogmarched through the throng into the weighing-room. Two minutes later he was back, by the same method, for the compulsory Coleman interview. Then it was the press conference, the champagne and a rather hurried, disorientated change into civilian suit.

One by one, the losers were trailing back. Inconspicuous, almost unnoticed amid the excitement, they slipped quietly into the weighing-room wearing looks which ranged from distress to anger to sheer relief.

O'Neill somehow still managed to be smiling, despite his well-fancied ride on Another Dolly having got him no farther than Bechers on the first circuit. The champion-elect, then, had still not completed a National in six attempts.

Jenny Hembrow contrived to look happy and sad simultaneously—happy that Sandwilan had given her such an unforgettable ride to the 19th fence, sad that her dream had ended there when Prince Rock refused, baulked her and prevented her making the jump. 'All I wanted was to get round,' she said. But at least she had proved that women are capable of it.

Steve Smith-Eccles looked grimmer than ever after Zongalero's failure, Richard Linley was bruised and unsmiling, and Irish amateur Aidan O'Connell, who rode with a stone overweight, was distinctly upset that his bid had ended at the relatively innocuous 23rd fence.

Amazingly, despite the fact that only four of the 30 starters finished, there were no serious injuries, either to horses or jockeys.

The next race was underway while some jockeys were still returning from their National efforts, but Fenwick was already planning a party. Surrounded by American friends and relations, he discussed tactics with the two men who had done most to make it all possible, trainer Captain Tim Forster and former champion jockey Graham Thorner.

Thorner's retirement in December, fully discussed earlier, had not precluded his interest in racing, and more particularly in Fenwick and Ben Nevis. He disclosed after the race that he had even retained his jockey's licence for the single reason that he would have been prepared to stand in on Ben Nevis if anything had happened to the American.

The only thing that happened to him that night was a hangover. Sleepless, yet still smiling and smartly suited, he led the horse back to Forster's stables at a village near Wantage the following morning.

Almost 500 people were there to welcome him, just as they had been eight years earlier, when the victorious horse was Well to Do—and the jockey was Thorner.

I spoke to Thorner on the Sunday afternoon and he sounded dreadful. 'I must have pneumonia,' he declared with mournful confidence. 'We were up all night, we've watched the video of the race about fifty times and drunk the place out of beer and coffee. I didn't feel right yesterday, but it's a lot worse now.'

Thorner, however, is not known for being wordless and he fought off his symptoms long enough to paint a graphic personal picture of the National victory. 'It may be unjust, but I feel part of it all. I've had as much pleasure from Charlie winning as I did from winning it myself. He is one of my greatest friends, and we spent hours talking about the race each time he was over here. We like the same things, Charlie and I, and we probably have very similar outlooks on life. He was absolutely dedicated to winning this race, even more so after falling last year, and he is the sort of fellow who will set his mind to something and keep working at it until he succeeds.

'Lots of people had lost all belief in Ben Nevis as a horse, but I always felt he had talent for this sort of race. But we were beginning to run short of excuses for him! Charlie has flown over from the States six times this season, and always stays at my house. He has been champion amateur back home, but that only entails about 15 rides a year—I used to ride that many in two or three days! I think he was a little shaken when he first came over and saw what English racing and English jockeys are all about, but if you knew how hard he has worked at it, you'd know why I like and admire him.

'We had a plan that he would just hunt round for the first circuit, but we obviously didn't expect him to be left clear so soon. Charlie may lack some of the finer points of jockeyship, but in those conditions yesterday all he needed was horsemanship—and he has plenty of that.

'He can go home and hold his head high now. Last year, you see, he went back and everyone started comparing him to Charlie Smith, the last American to win the race 15 years ago. He would have hated to go back again and have people say he had failed to conquer it like Smith did.'

So Charlie Fenwick did fly home, on the Monday, to his city office, his wife and three children and, no doubt, the makings of another new challenge. The 29 British jockeys he beat were left to count their bruises and wait for another year.

The Professional's National—Jeff King

Jeff King spent the morning of the 1980 Grand National playing golf— just as he had done before most of his previous 14 rides in Britain's richest, roughest steeplechase. King had more experience of Aintree's

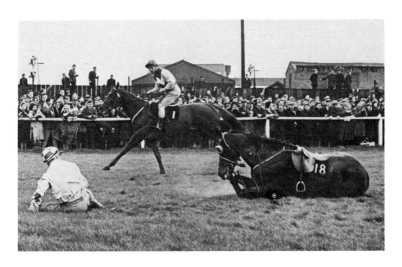

TOP: Less than 48 hours after a serious car crash, King took his ride in the 1966 Grand National … and here, aboard the Japanese-bred Fujino-O, has time to spare a sympathetic glance for Willie Robinson, who has fallen from his own mount's stable companion.

ABOVE: Two old hands in the ring before the 1975 Grand National. King rode Money Market, which finished fourth, Irishman Tommy Carberry was on the winner, L'Escargot.

121

Cheeks puffed out in characteristic style, Jeff King and Casamayor clear the infamous Chair in the 1980 National. Camera angle and the battering from previous horses make the fence look almost tame, but don't be fooled.

fences than any other jockey in this year's race, yet the most he had to show for it was a third place on Rondetto in 1968. 'You need all your birthdays in one afternoon to win the National,' he had once told me—and up to now such a freak had not occurred in King's life.

The years had not been without incident, however, and indelibly printed on King's memory is an extraordinary tale of events leading up to the 1966 race. He had accepted the ride on a Japanese-bred animal, trained by Fulke Walwyn, and was anything but sanguine about his chances of success. Just a few days before the Liverpool meeting, Fred Winter contacted King and offered him a far better ride—a horse called Anglo. King, however, was aware that Tim Norman, a close friend, had previously been asked to ride the horse, and declined Winter's offer on ethical grounds. When the meeting began, a number of jockeys were, as usual, staying at Southport, and after racing on the Thursday King had a car-load of passengers for the 15-mile drive to the hotel. Among them was Tim Norman.

The shortest route from Aintree to Southport takes in a suicidally narrow swing bridge on a less than salubrious housing estate, and it was near here that King and car came to grief, hit side on by a vehicle coming the opposite way.

'The car was a complete wreck,' he recalls, 'and I think I was barely conscious. Tim was in the back, and he managed to climb clear by way of the window. The next thing I remember is a voice saying "They're all OK except Kingy … I think he's dead". It was John Gamble, another jockey, who had come up behind us with Josh Gifford. Between them, they managed to get me out, but I was taken to hospital by ambulance.'

King was released later than night, and took his place in the National. So too did Norman, although neither man could claim to have been fully fit. At a range of 14 years, King struggles to remember the name of the horse he rode. He does, however, recall very clearly that Tim Norman won the National on the horse which had been offered to him.

A perennial hazard of jockeys engaged for the National is the risk of injury in an earlier race during the Liverpool meeting. It happens all too often—Tommy Carberry being the prime sufferer in 1980—and it happened to King in 1968. Booked to ride Rondetto again in the National—he rode him four times in all—he fell heavily in the Topham Trophy, run over the National course, on the Thursday.

'It shook me up a bit, but the most inconvenient part of it was that I was left with a raging black eye. If I looked straight ahead with my eyes on the level, I could not see a thing out of one of them.

'These days, with stricter controls over medical fitness, it is feasible that I would have been stopped from riding in the National, but my view was that it was a hindrance and annoyance to me, but not a danger to other riders. I went ahead, and spent the entire race peering up like a short-sighted old man. Funnily enough, that was the year I finished third.'

In 14 National rides, King had naturally endured his share of falls and more than his quota of disappointments. Now, in 1980, he was to ride Casamayor, bred in Argentina, trained by Peter Bailey and very much a long shot in the eyes of the bookies. Four days before the race, Mecca were offering 100 to 1, but by Saturday they had joined the majority of other major firms in quoting 50s.

King had decided in favour of Casamayor despite the fact that he was also asked to ride Another Dolly for Fred Rimell. Jonjo O'Neill subsequently took that mount, and the horse was backed down to 12 to 1. But King remained convinced that he had made the correct choice.

Privately, he confided his opinion that Another Dolly was not the type of horse which would prosper at Liverpool's unique obstacles, and that he would be very surprised if he completed the course. He was right, too, but Casamayor, although surviving for appreciably longer, also failed to make it.

For King, the routine of National week has been settled for many years. He takes his wife, Maureen, to Liverpool—the only meeting she will attend in the course of a season—and the Royal Hotel is an essential tradition. This year, the Kings arrived early on Thursday afternoon, although Jeff had no rides booked for that day. By five o'clock, they were installed in their hotel room, and Jeff was about to be interviewed by the bogus maintenance man over the state of his teasmade ...

'Ever since I have been coming to Liverpool for the National, we have stayed at The Royal. It has some hazards—its plumbing has been faulty in the past and the service is sometimes less than speedy—but I don't think Aintree week would feel the same if we went anywhere else. Maureen enjoys Southport, too, and she always spends the Friday shopping with a friend, before coming to the course on the Saturday.

'I'm not the type to have any superstitions about staying in the same room—no room has ever brought me luck here, anyway—but we always seem to be situated in the same area of the hotel, with a large, high-ceilinged room overlooking the seafront. I found it very relaxing, but Maureen always complained at having to walk down the corridor to have a bath. These days, we always manage a room with a private bathroom.

'This year, we spent both Thursday and Friday evening at a Spanish restaurant down the road from the hotel. Some jocks have to be very careful what they eat before the National, but I have very rarely had to do light, and this year I had 10 st. 12 lb.—6lb. above my normal weight. So, without any worries, I enjoyed big, three-course dinners both evenings.

'I had a few glasses of wine each night, and a beer or two. It was sensible drinking. I am fit enough to shake off the effects the next morning anyway. Liverpool is a very sociable meeting, and I have seen jockeys absolutely stoned on the Friday night—and ride the winner the next day!

'Golf is as much a part of the week as racing for me. In the past, I have played on Thursday and Friday nights as well as Saturday morning, but this year I only managed the one round. It has become a very expensive game, and I begrudge paying £8 for nine holes as you have to at many clubs.

'I was going to play on Friday morning at Formby, but I woke up to the sound of rain lashing against the window, so gave it up as a bad job and stayed in bed well past my normal rising time. I enjoyed lingering over the papers, having a leisurely bath, and then putting on my suit and going down to see some hungover expressions in the bar.

'Maureen had gone off on her shopping expedition, and I was at a loose end until it was time to leave for the races. Bottles of champagne were being bought as if they were the last ones in Liverpool, but a drinking session was the last thing I needed, so I only accepted a polite half-glass before walking out into the dampness of the morning in search of a new hat. My old felt trilby had seen me through 15 seasons—almost back to my first National ride—and had now developed a hole. Dunns provided me with a suitable substitute ... I hope this one lasts another 15 years.

'The rain was resting for a couple of hours, but the going was officially heavy, unofficially desperate. The second race of the day was a selling hurdle, and there was such a torrential downpour that even the television cameras could hardly pick out the horses. My spirits sank, as Casamayor needed good ground to retain a real chance. The same applied to my two rides that day, and neither produced more than the £32 fee. At least I was sure of earning a good fee for the National— offered by the horse's owner and traditionally done only at Aintree.

'By the end of racing, the sun was shining, but much more rain would undoubtedly put the National at risk. Several riders went out to walk the course, but that did not appeal. I could get all the exercise I wanted on the golf course.

'Another Spanish meal was followed by a few drinks in the bar, which grew steadily noisier as the other racegoing residents returned from their evenings out. I stayed up until half-past-one, then went to bed and left Maureen to enjoy herself.

'There is never any point in me going to bed early. I am a light and restless sleeper and don't need more than about six hours each night. Even if I go up at midnight, it is invariably an hour or more before I drop off, and even then I generally toss and turn most of the night.

'I'm told I've always been this way, and Maureen certainly confirms that I have never slept well since we've been married. I also used to sleep-walk quite regularly and the first time Maureen saw it, she was frightened to death. She tells me I once wandered into our son's room and picked him out of his cot. Maureen was annoyed and told me to go back to bed as I'd woken David. I did so, and could remember nothing about it the next morning.

'On another occasion, I apparently got out of bed in nothing but my pyjama tops and walked dreamily into the bathroom, and from there into the spare room, where I attempted to get into bed with our babysitter. She screamed enough to get me back to the right room—but I insist I knew nothing of that when I woke, either.

'There are jockeys who say they sleep badly before the National, but by my standards I had a good night and was up at 7.30 a.m. to get on the golf course at Ormskirk. It was freezing cold, but relaxing as ever. I didn't think about the race at all, until I was back in the car on the way to the course.

'The traffic was worse than I've ever known it, with almost all of it being diverted down the side-street which leads to the owners, trainers and jockeys' car park. We were queuing for ages, but it didn't matter as I'd left ample time. If I had cut it much finer, I'd have had to get out and run—and I've known that happen to many jockeys before now!

'My ride in the first race was a lost cause as the horse is hopeless on heavy going and was only being run because his owner had flown from Ireland to watch. I pulled him up before the end, and by the time I got back to the weighing-room there was an hour left before the National.

'Perhaps it is me getting old, but I felt there was less atmosphere than in past years. There is normally plenty of larking about going on, but I sensed it was very much quieter this year. John Francome was as cool and as funny as ever, but some were pretty subdued.

'There will always be tension evident before any big race, and at my stage of a career, I don't feel any more for the National. But I'm sure that some do, if only because there is so much at stake. I'm often asked if I'm aware of the television cameras' presence, or of the size of the crowd, but to be honest I never notice at all, even at Liverpool. It would be too simplistic to say the National is just another race, because it is far more than that. But the pre-race routine is pretty much the same.

'It is always wise to have some sort of race-plan for Aintree, if only because the field is so enormous. Peter Bailey had advised me to lay up well behind the leaders if possible, but knowing that Casamayor is an unpredictable old thing, just to be prepared to ride him as he is going. I tracked John Francome on Rough and Tumble, and was close enough as we went over Bechers the first time.

'Another Dolly fell there, but he was on the far side of the course from me, and I wasn't aware he had gone at all. Of course, I didn't want either the horse or Jonjo to be hurt, but it was gratifying to be proved right. I would have been sick if he'd won.

'To my mind, they had all gone off far too quickly from the start. The ground was the worst I have ever known at Liverpool—by a long way—and it was plain suicide to race round the first circuit. Several horses had had enough by the time we jumped the Chair, which is the 14th of 30. Early in the race, everyone is intent on finding some light and space for themselves, but after jumping three or four, you invariably find yourself upsides someone and you might well have a quick chat between jumps—not much, just a question as to how he is going, probably. But once we had taken Canal Turn, the going got even worse, and my horse would not run at all. I dropped back last, and had nobody to talk to even if I'd wanted to.

'It was as we came up past the stands that Casamayor began to run well again. I went past three or four and the horse actually took a hold of the bridle and began to pull. I had to hold him back, as it was too soon to think about getting up to the leaders—but even then, I knew deep down that we would have a hell of a job surviving through the stickiest of the ground.

'As things turned out, we didn't get that far. He took off all wrong at the 19th, hit it hard—and that was the end of it for another year. It was disappointing, of course, but I wasn't very surprised in the conditions. If he had fallen on good ground, I would have felt very upset because, despite what the bookies' thought, I always felt he was a Liverpool horse with a very fair chance of getting round.

'Seven horses had come to grief at that fence, and the one lady rider, Jenny Hembrow, was among them. I had lost my horse—I later learned that he had fallen, riderless, at Bechers, so I hopped up behind Jenny and had a lift back to the unsaddling enclosure. She was pretty upset, as another horse had blocked her and put her out of the race when she was going well.

'A number of trainers were wandering around the front of the weighing-room when we got back, still trying to find out what had happened to their horses. Peter Bailey met me and had no idea that both Casamayor and Prince Rock, his other entry, had got no further than the 19th.

'In the weighing-room, the first thing we always try to discover is if anyone was hurt. This year, as 26 failed to finish, that was a more difficult task than ever, but in fact Richard Linley, who had taken a kick in the chest, was the only rider with anything approaching a serious injury. Andy Turnell and I had both hurt our legs—nothing much but enough to prevent us riding again that day.

'When Charlie Fenwick came in on Ben Nevis, he was hustled into the weighing-room by two policemen and then straight back out again for a television interview. I don't know Charlie very well, so would hardly have been involved in the celebrating too closely. But we didn't see him again for the best part of an hour and, as usual, the whole thing became an anti-climax.

'Lots of people said this was a sub-standard National and perhaps they are right. But I would not want that to detract from either the winner or Rough and Tumble. Both are genuine, staying horses ideally suited to the National, and they did their jobs admirably.

'With nothing to keep me at the course, I wasn't sorry to slip away before the last race. Maureen and I were back in Cirencester, at the hotel which regularly has our National night dinner custom, soon after seven, and back home in time to see the race again on television. It didn't change my opinion one bit. I'm still pleased I rode Casamayor, and would ride him again, given the choice. But time is running out for me, now, and I suppose I have begun to accept that I will probably never feature among the National winners.'

The Amateur's National—Brod Munro-Wilson

There were those who chuckled into their champagne when Broderick Munro-Wilson slid ignominiously off the back of Coolishall soon after the third fence in the National. Plenty of I-told-you-so's no doubt got busy pouring scorn on the riding ability of this most enigmatic amateur.

For the sneerers and the cynics, found on every racecourse, Mr B. Munro-Wilson is something of a sitting target. Double-barrelled name, public-school and Cambridge education, merchant banker and, to top the image, a gangling figure and tea-on-the-lawn accent foreign to most jockeys. Every credential, in fact, for the knockers to roll round their tongues and relish.

To be frank, Brod's riding style has won some harsh words from the professionals, too, but the one thing none can deny he possesses is boundless enthusiasm—a quality cruelly treated by the manner of his dismissal from the race he had convinced himself he could win.

Aluminium stirrups were never meant to shatter, much less in four places simultaneously. Yet that was the fate of the hapless Munro-Wilson—at the very first fence, to boot. He cleared two more, the first with one foot in the remaining intact iron, the second without stirrups at all, and was then gently and inevitably unshipped.

He returned to the weighing-room brandishing the offending object and was still there several hours later, disconsolately brooding over his unfortunate end.

Brod owned and trained Coolishall himself, one of 12 horses in the small yet efficient yard adjoining his Sussex home. It is the sort of place that could comfortably adorn the cover of *Country Life*—15th century, oak-beamed, with three storeys, more rooms than I could quickly count, an outhouse/cottage of similar vintage and even an all-weather paddock.

An individualist and adventurer by nature, he studied economics at university and now has his own banking business, perhaps concluding only two or three deals a year, but always in figures like telephone numbers. For the duration of the 1979–80 National Hunt season, however, Brod relegated business to Wednesdays only and elevated horses to his number one priority. He was up at 6.30 a.m. most mornings, rode out two or three horses either side of breakfast, then assisted his staff of three around the stables.

He rides most of his own horses, very occasionally engaging a professional for schooling purposes, and is distinctive as much for his height above the saddle as for his riding colours of chocolate, with yellow spots.

The dangers of the sport concern him little, as one might expect of a man who serves in the SAS and has undergone some of the most severe military training imaginable, notably one awesome exercise in a Welsh mountain blizzard when, he admits: 'I thought I had had my lot—I was constantly falling in drifts which came up to my chin'.

Despite the unavoidable falls, Brod had suffered no serious injuries from racing, other than a broken wrist, sustained in a Saturday point-to-point meeting. He was scheduled to ride a hotly-backed favourite, Champers Galore, at Plumpton on the Monday and was so confident of victory and determined to claim his share of it that he had the wrist set and plastered in London that morning, camouflaged the plaster under the sleeve of his silks and went out to ride.

The price of the horse lengthened as his handicap was noticed, but Champers Galore still won comfortably to reward his rider's rather reckless brand of courage.

Coolishall was bought with the Grand National in mind, having already completed the course once, to finish fourth in 1978, and fallen in 1979. With every passing day before the race, Broderick's confidence appeared to increase. He had no other rides at the Liverpool meeting, but set off for Aintree on the Wednesday afternoon, sharing the driving of his modern, well-equipped horse-box with his head-lad, Bernie ...

'It's a long run from Sussex, but motorway for much of the route, and we were able to do a steady 65 mph. We took along Beeno, another of my hunter chasers, purely as company for Coolie—they get on very well together. Our box can be made into a mobile home with sleeping quarters if ever I want it, and it also has a stereo tape player. We had music on for the entire journey and I believe the horses really enjoy it.

'Bernie naturally stays near the racecourse yard with the horse, in the stable-lads hostel, but I had booked into the Adelphi in Liverpool and was very much looking forward to it. I had not stayed at the Adelphi for 17 years, when I had spent a night there before my pre-Cambridge round-the-world trip. It is the only hotel in England which still has linen sheets on the beds. Nothing much had changed.

'I was up at 6.00 a.m. on Thursday morning, and at Aintree by dawn. During the National meeting, one is only allowed to work horses on the course between seven and eight in the morning, which makes this uncivilised time of starting essential. Coolie was sensationally good in his work, and I began to believe that things were going our way.

'My breakfast consisted of coffee, black, with a cigar. Lester Piggott always reckons that coffee and cigars help him lose weight, so why shouldn't I try? My National weight was 10st. 6lb., which is more than a stone and a half less than my normal living weight. For weeks past, I'd been wasting, eating only one meal a day and restricting that to plain meat and citrus fruits. The only indulgence I allowed myself was chocolate for energy. I knew I would not quite make the weight, but I was confident of being only three or four pounds over the top.

'Even on Thursday, the unique National atmosphere was very evident. Everyone is so very friendly during this meeting. They all know it is the big one of the season and there is a feeling almost of reverence. I have even noticed that there is not as much swearing and cursing in the weighing-room as usual!

'That night, I took Bernie out to dinner in the restaurant at the top of Liverpool's Post Office Tower. Some of these places are gimmicky, but the food was very good at this one. Bernie could indulge in a steak au poivre, with thick pepper sauce, but I had to restrict myself to a plain steak. Coolishall had settled in and was eating up well, we felt sure he knew where he was, and we concluded that we were as prepared as possible.

'My morning routine was the same on Friday—early start, riding out on the course, and trying to sweat off a few more ounces by wearing as many layers of clothes as I could squeeze on.

'I wanted to be certain that all my tack was in order, so in mid-morning I took the lot into the weighing-room and asked the valet to check through it. It was ironic that the stirrups had a thorough check—but quite insignificant because we could have tested them with a sledgehammer and nothing would have snapped.

'There were a lot of unhappy people when the heavens opened during racing that afternoon, but I was delighted. Coolie absolutely loves the heavy going, and I reckoned that applied to very few others in the race. Lord Oaksey saw me at the height of the rain-storm and said he thought it was great weather for Coolie. Maybe too much went in our favour, I don't know—I remember Bernie said, after the race: 'The trouble was, everything was too perfect!'

'Bernie and I walked the entire National course that evening, and it was then that I formulated the race-plan. Someone said to me as we were lining up at the start the next day, that I looked very relaxed. Well, I felt it—because I knew exactly what I wanted to do, fence by fence.

'My plan was to take up position on the unfashionable far right of the field to avoid trouble, and to let Coolie take a hold—as he loves to do—for the first couple of fences. I wanted to keep to the right of the course for a complete circuit, and only switch to the inside as we went out into the country for the second time. But it all came to nothing, of course ...

'I saw Coolie at evening stables and was pleased to see how well he was eating. They sense that they are at the races, which is why I had brought him up so early to allow him every chance to settle. Josh Gifford's horses were next door and were apparently hardly eating at all.

'Back at the hotel, my mother and other relatives had arrived, and a number of good luck cards and telegrams. Some were from friends in the city, and I was particularly touched by a card from Martin O'Halloran, who rode Coolie when he finished fourth in 1978 and would have done again last year but for falling ill on the day of the race.

'I think I was the only jockey staying at the Adelphi, although Fred Rimell the trainer was there. The press had caught on to my horse by this time, and the hotel staff were more openly excited than I was. They were all opening doors for me—and the porters even shone my boots that night.

'A piece of chicken and a glass of orange juice was my dinner, and I turned in for a very early night. I had booked a wake-up call for 5.30 a.m., as usual, so when the phone rang, I just assumed that must be the time. I didn't bother to answer it, but got up, dashed into the bathroom and started shaving. There was a knock at the door, and when I opened it, a porter handed me a telegram. I thanked him and asked him to have my taxi ready. "Why do you want a taxi, sir," he asked. "It's only half-past twelve!"

'After that rather amusing interruption, I slept pretty well, woke with the real alarm call and got to the course in time to give Coolie a gentle four-furlong pipe-opener. We saw several members of the opposition, incuding Zongalero, and Coolie had a good sniff at them.

'I allowed myself a scrambled egg, without toast, and some black coffee, and even accepted half-a-glass of champagne from a couple of journalists. Then, at ten, I went upstairs to soak in a hot bath for an hour.

'It was extraordinary. I was not a bit nervous. On the Friday morning, the valets had been pulling my leg, saying they knew I would be a bag of nerves before the race—and I had to admit that my heart was beating a bit faster than usual. But on the day itself, with everything planned in my mind, I was completely composed and relaxed.

'I was interviewed by David Coleman at two o'clock, then spent some time watching the other interviews, and the early races, on the weighing-room television. There is a snack bar there, and I was one who indulged in half a cup of tea. We all groaned when Jonjo, who never has weight worries, supped two large cups of tea with milk and sugar.

'At the weigh-in, I could have managed ten-eight, but I was advised to use a decent breast-girth and accept the extra two pounds. Despite all the sweating and wasting, I have rarely felt better. I was fit enough to have gone in the ring with Cassius Clay.

'It was a struggle to get out to the parade ring. We almost had to fight through the crowds, and once there, found the ring far too small for a 30-runner race. It was chaotic, with jockeys and horses thundering in every direction.

'Everything went perfectly to plan at first. I got just the position I wanted on the right-hand rails, and Coolie made a super start. Richard Rowe was upsides me on Josh Gifford's Mannyboy, and I saw him fall at the first out of the corner of my eye. Coolie had made a marvellous leap, but either in mid-air, or just as we landed, there was a noise like the firing of a gun. I shall never forget it, no matter how many more races I ride in. The sudden realisation that my left foot was swinging loose was a dreadful shock. I jumped the second with my right foot in the iron, but realised that was hopeless. I took the third without stirrups, and although Coolie sailed over it, there was no way I could stay on.

'I had grazed my head slightly, but it was nothing to worry about. I got up and wandered onto the tarmac at the side of the track. I just could not believe it. I felt that it couldn't really have happened, that it was just some horrible nightmare and I would wake up to find myself back at the start.

'At first, I couldn't see Coolie, and then I picked him out, the one with the sheepskin nose-band, hopping over the fences with ridiculous ease. As I watched him jump round, I felt as if I was standing outside my own life, looking in. Incredulity, amazement and growing despondency were my chief fighting emotions.

'There was nothing for it but to walk back, with the sinking knowledge that I would have to answer dozens of questions as to what had happened. The best thing was finding the shattered iron—I at least had the proof for any who may have doubted.

'Bernie caught Coolie as he ran past the Stands. He had jumped the Chair quite superbly, was plainly enjoying himself and showed his annoyance at being taken out of the race by trying to kick down his stable-door.

'On getting back to the weighing-room, the first thing I did was grab a cup of tea with sugar and milk, and a huge piece of fruit cake. It was over, there was no point in worrying any more—and anyway, I always eat ravenously when I become anguished about anything.

'As the other riders trooped back in, everyone began asking everyone else for their own stories. For mine, I just held up the

In a matter of minutes, Brod Munro-Wilson's dream was to be shattered – along with his stirrup iron. Coolishall, being led round before the off at Aintree.

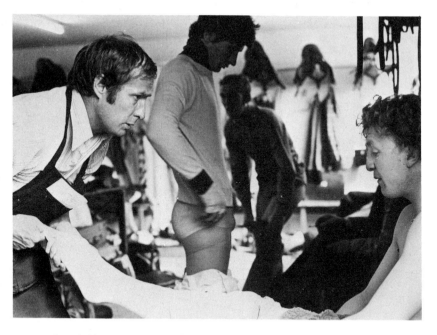

Intent in his post-race jobs, John Buckingham, one-time Grand National hero, now the unseen
essential, the valet. Brian Smart is the jockey being attended.

smashed stirrup. It was the best explanation I had, and said more than any words. They were all very nice about it—they knew what a big personal effort I had put into the race, to make the weight and get everything right. I know a number of the pros would have liked the ride on Coolie themselves, but that didn't stop them being sympathetic now.

'Charlie Fenwick came in—Chewing-gum Charlie as I called him— and of course, the champagne was opened. There is never any bad feeling after a National. In other races, there may be some mumblings and moanings about the winner, but at Aintree, everyone accepts that whoever gets there deserves every accolade going.

'I changed back into street clothes, then walked back on to the course with a pal. I had some weird idea that we may find the sheered-off piece of aluminium, yet didn't really expect to. But as soon as we reached the landing point, my pal saw it. At least he saw one, and then a second piece. Still, the jigsaw wasn't complete, and it was only then that I realised the iron had snapped in four different places. I found the final piece myself, and my mother later said we should mount them all, set in perspex, to remind us that covering every human element is not always enough.

'We ate a subdued dinner at the hotel, then watched the race again on television at 10.30 p.m. It made me feel even worse, watching the horse jump round so easily without me. The following morning, we sneaked back onto the National course with both Coolie and Beeno, and jumped them over the last two National fences. Coolie was just like a bird, he devoured the fences with consumate ease. Bernie turned to me and said "Guv'nor, we have been robbed".

'I am an optimist, and I shall keep fighting on. But I felt so sorry for Bernie, who had done so much work to make sure the horse was spot on. Our only consolation is that we share the knowledge, privately, that we do have the best Grand National horse in the country. I only hope he gets the chance to prove it next year.'

The Valet's National—John Buckingham

John Buckingham is a fixture at the National. Jockeys may come and go but, in the recent past and foreseeable future, the weighing-room will always contain this short, kindly man with receding hair, boundless energy and overalls which evoke more thoughts of butchery than horse-racing. Buckingham never rides now—he gave that up almost a decade ago—but he could, if the pride ever swelled within him and the moment arose, tell most of his jockey friends a thing or two about getting round the National course.

In fact, there is not a boastful inch of Buckingham, who retired from riding in 1971 having won the most sensational of all Nationals and completed the course three more times in three attempts.

Buckingham was the pilot of Foinavon, labelled the milk-cart horse in the build-up to the 1967 race, yet a household name by Saturday evening after steering unerringly through unprecedented carnage at the 23rd fence to run on and win at 100 to 1. For a week, perhaps a month, Buckingham shared the celebrity billing with his mount. He enjoyed the usual champagne and stardom interviews, appeared live on Sunday Night at the London Palladium and, in all probability, was even offered a few more spare rides on the strength of his triumph.

Memories are short, however, and Buckingham, hampered by a broken arm the following year, made a hasty descent of the jockey league. True, his Aintree record was exemplary, and he even completed the course in 1971 by remounting after Limeburner had fallen at the second last when contesting third place. But a jockey cannot, despite popular opinion, live by the National alone, and the shortage of rides was driving Buckingham close to despair.

In the 1970–71 season, he rode only one winner. He was 31 and if the racing game was about to discard him, had little idea of a new vocation. Coming from a farming family, he had left school at 16 and chosen to be a stable-lad in preference to a shepherd, despite the unusual fact that he had never ridden a horse in his life. Now, after 15 years, a marriage and an imminent child, he was virtually redundant.

He thought of trying to set up as a trainer, but knew that the financial commitment made the scheme a non-starter. Then a quiet approach from an official of the Jockey Association opened the way for Buckingham to stay in jump-racing in a manner he had never considered.

'They needed another valet, and offered me the job. To be honest, it didn't take very long to make up my mind because I really don't know what I would have done otherwise. And it's a decision I have never regretted for a moment.'

Broadly speaking, the duties of the valets are to provide everything their jockeys will need in the way of tack, colours, etc.—and at the right time. The operation is a masterpiece of planning, using the racecard—which shows the jockeys and their relevant colours in each race—and organising the room and the day accordingly.

The valets also wash and polish all the jockeys' tack and, if required, transport it—along with a mountain of their own equipment—between meetings. Buckingham often looks after 20 riders a day.

For these services, Buckingham, his brother Tom who 'works' the southern courses with him, and a small private company who look after the north, charge each jockey a fee. They pay the valet for each ride they have, on a descending scale which starts at £3.50 for one, and is then reduced to £2 for the second and £1 for the rest. The fees were recently increased enough to persuade some jockeys that they would be better and richer looking after themselves. Andy Turnell and Richard Evans are two who now decline the convenience of the valet and, for their pains, are obliged to change at one end of the weighing-room on each course, staying well away from the valets' patch.

By the very fact of their constant presence, the valets are in a unique position to study the moods and habits of their charges, and Buckingham has no doubt that he would struggle to find a more agreeable breed of men. He does, however, feel that there are less characters about than in his riding days.

'Fifteen years ago, almost every jock seemed to be a joker. There were two who stood out, Jimmy Morrissey and Dave Sunderland, and there was scarcely a day passed when they were not up to some mischief. I remember Dave at Plumpton one day, deliberately leaping onto a seat by an open window, in the nude, just as a policewoman walked by.

'Jeff King and John Francome are probably the two great characters among the southern riders these days. They are always looking for a new story to tell. Several times during every meeting, I'll see a group of jockeys gathered in a huddle in a corner of the weighing-room. It'll be nothing serious—just someone telling a dirty joke.

'Some of the young ones are up to tricks, too. At Windsor one day this year, Graham McCourt cut the crutch out of Richard Floyd's underpants, while Richard was out riding in a race. When he came back, he sat around for a while, not hurrying to change despite everyone subtly urging him to get on with it. Eventually, it was time for the riders to go out for the next race, but no-one would leave the room until Richard had started dressing and made the discovery.'

Buckingham also sees the stress and tension attached to the game, heightened as the National approaches. 'I have heard jockeys say it is no different to any other race. Well that is a lot of rubbish. It is the toughest race in the world and the most famous—two reasons why it has to be different.'

It is early Thursday morning when Buckingham's National begins. His estate car crammed with tack of all sizes and descriptions, he drives from his neat, estate house in a village near Banbury, up the motorway to Liverpool.

Not for the valets the luxury of the Adelphi, or even the old-world charm of the Royal Clifton. Just like cricket umpires, they find some cheap, comfortable digs near the racecourse. John has stayed in the same digs for years and has no complaints.

If there were no other differences from the run-of-the-mill meetings, Buckingham says he would still know it was National week for one perennial reason.

'Most of the jockeys come to me, either on Thursday or Friday, and ask me to check their saddles or their colours. I do the job for them every day of the season and they never worry at all. But this is the National, and that is just a sign of the nerves which affect everyone here.

'On the Saturday, the tension is impossible to miss. Jump jockeys always mess about in the weighing-room but at Liverpool it is different altogether. There is much more laughing and joking than usual, a lot of it forced as a camouflage for the butterflies.

'People say Cheltenham is a bigger, better meeting and it certainly does have some atmosphere. But it is nothing to Liverpool. You can feel the tension there. Let's face it, it is a hell of a strain. Most of the riders will have been thinking about the race for days, worrying about it like they will for no other event in the season.'

On National morning, John breakfasted at his digs and was at the course by 8.30 a.m. For him, too, the National still breeds a kind of tension, an urge to get things exactly right.

'I like to check and recheck everything. I take a pride in making sure that every saddle and every boot belonging to my jockeys is absolutely shining for the National.

'By 9.30 a.m., there were a surprising amount of people about. The caterers had moved into their quarters to prepare for the invasion, and the broadcasters' technicians were setting up equipment. Some of the jockeys had been on the course earlier, riding out their National horses, but for a while at least, the valets had the weighing-room to themselves.

'I wasn't feeling too great by this time. I had a bit of a pain around my ears and recalled that my daughters had both had mumps recently. But I was sure I'd had it before, so didn't worry. The doctor had a look and said I probably had a throat infection ... but I knew it wasn't that.

'At Aintree, most of the jocks arrive much earlier than usual. On a normal day, they would not get to the course until an hour before the first. But on National day, several were there by 11.30 a.m. Phil Blacker and Steve Smith-Eccles were among the first, but I was too busy to notice who else was arriving.

'Friday had been so wet that it had been impossible to get all the tack clean that evening, so there was a lot of soaping up to finish before all the tack could be hung in the right place.

'As the riders all came in, sat down, and had however much tea they could allow themselves, I missed Bryan Smart. Jocking him off his National ride 24 hours before the race was one of the cruellest things I have seen in racing. The lad loves Liverpool more than most, I've noticed over the years, and I could tell he was heartbroken. He said little, but the expression on his face was enough.

'The Aintree weighing-room is split into two. The meeting used to be mixed, so that the flat jockeys used one half and the jumpers the other, but now that it is all jumping it makes our job easier. Most of the lads wander from room to room while they are changing, and there was the usual amount of nervous tension on view. I think it's partly down to the race being at Aintree, which holds no other meetings now. You only walk into that weighing-room once a year, and that once is for National week.

'John Francome, as ever, was incredibly cool—nothing ever seems to disturb him—and I noticed that Charlie Fenwick was very quiet. He is a pleasant bloke, Charlie, but not the type to joke about. He just came in, sat in his place and changed. Funnily enough, I had put a few bob on Ben Nevis the previous year and fancied him a fair bit. But that morning, Tim Forster had come into the weighing-room and said the ground would kill him.

'By the time we have got all the jockeys fixed up, and they have walked out for the National, there is no time for us to get any sort of viewing place, so we always watch the race on television in the weighing-room. The place was packed as ever, mainly with people who had left it too late to get into the stands.

'As usual, it was complete chaos afterwards. I took Charlie's saddle from him and didn't see him again for ages. Graham Thorner asked me to get some champagne for the lads, so I went off to collect it, and by the time I got back, a lot of the other riders were returning.

'There is no great gnashing of teeth or weeping. Being the National, everyone accepts that the chances of winning are pretty minimal, and that they can get brought down by something, however good their own horse may be. Steve Smith-Eccles, whose mount had been ante-post favourite, actually came back and said he was glad it was all over.

'Our job never becomes an anti-climax afterwards, because there are three more races for us to do. That night, I was in the weighing-room until 6.30 p.m. By then, I had had enough. I didn't feel very well and, although most of the washing had not been done, I just packed it all in the car and got on the motorway.

'It had been a hard meeting. At other courses, I might lie down on a bench and have a kip for 20 minutes between races, but at Liverpool I can never keep still. If I get a few minutes free, I walk out of the weighing-room to soak up a bit of atmosphere. I never actually see a race, other than on television, but I enjoy watching the people.'

Buckingham went back home that night, to his memories of 1967, his Grand National trophy nestling on top of his sideboard, and the almost inevitable paintings of horse and rider which seem to adorn the front-room walls of most jockeys. He may well have played the video of the 1967 race again, just as he has done so many times before (he once even took it to show a local women's institute), but by bed-time his ailments had worsened and by Monday the fear was confirmed. John had mumps.

Two who missed out—Evans and Champion
Among the millions who watched the Grand National, on the course and at home on television were two jockeys too concerned with their own problems to fully relish the occasion.

Richard Evans' handicap was straightforward. Nine days before the

National, at Devon and Exeter, his left foot had twisted in his iron as his mount fell. He was treated on the course, a sprained ankle was diagnosed and, after taking a lift with John Burke to a Bristol service station where he had parked his own car, he drove home to Stratford.

The pain increased with each mile, which was hardly surprising. Evans had broken his ankle. Just how much further damage may have been caused it is impossible to assess, but when the plaster was put on two days later, he was given a compulsory six weeks of moody moping. Evans is not normally one to languish in the melancholy of his own misfortune. A friendly and industrious man, he is one of the most sociable members of the jockey circuit. But this was different.

Already during the season, Evans had missed several weeks of racing after distressing falls. He had not ridden many winners when he returned, either, and would have been resigned to another unspectacular close to the season but for the stimulant of the National, just around the corner.

As usual, he had been due to ride The Pilgarlic, Fred Rimell's remarkable hunter-chaser. For three successive years, Evans and 'The Pill' had finished in the first five. It was a partnership which continued to astound the bookies with its success, and Evans had grown to look forward to it each year. Now the ride went to Ron Hyett and Evans could not conceal his hope that the horse failed to improve enough to win.

Anything but a vindictive man, Evans could be excused for being a reluctant well-wisher on this occasion. Not getting a National ride is bad enough. Getting a good one and losing it is a savage stroke of ill fortune and Evans, sitting at home in Stratford-upon-Avon on big-race day, was torn between pride in his old horse and bitterness at his own absence as The Pilgarlic, looking once more fit to stay forever, took fourth place in defiance of the treacherous going.

Bob Champion was an equally unwilling National spectator although for him, the worst of his agonies of pain and self-doubt had passed by this final Saturday in March. Cancer had attacked him suddenly in the early summer of 1979. He was operated upon in July and there followed the experience of chemotherapy treatment, a torment which only those who have been through it can conceive—and they rarely wish to relive it.

Champion emerged from all this, to a wild and windy Thursday in January when he was told he was cured. 'I'm perfectly all right now, always providing it doesn't come back of course,' he said later, with that hint of reserve which all such sufferers must feel.

'When I found out what I had got, I was petrified. But if my example helps other people in the same position to overcome their fears, then I am happy to discuss it now.'

Champion had been on the verge of high success as first jockey to

Josh Gifford, but for some time it had appeared he would never ride again, even if he conquered the illness. But determination, and the encouragement of his trainer and certain owners, took him to America, for, among other things, courses in body-building. Back in England, he announced himself fit and looking forward to the 1980–81 season.

'I want to get back to normal as quickly as possible—and that means riding as soon as I can. I don't want sympathy. I just want to be thought of as the same person I was before all this happened.

Both Richard Evans and Bob Champion felt a little detached from the revelries of National day, of course. But they at least knew they should be back next year, when it would undoubtedly be the turn of one or two other jockeys to feel the helplessness of being the frustrated stars of Aintree.

13 The bad and the ugly

Villainy

A number of years ago, a young northern jockey was making good progress towards establishing himself as a regular on the circuit. Whether he knew it or not, however, he was antagonising his more experienced colleagues by consistently trying to sneak up the inside on the bends and at the obstacles. Their retribution was harsh: several clubbed together to teach the boy a lesson. But their intended cane become a dagger on the downstroke.

On his now accustomed burst up the inner, the youngster was cut off by a sudden, rehearsed movement across the track by those in front. He was not just forced back, but put into the rails, trapping his inside leg with agonising effect. That young jockey never rode again. His leg was amputated in an emergency operation. Those who had put him in the theatre left the racecourse unaccused, unquestioned.

This story is told by Jeff King as a vivid example of the human dangers which can often complement the static ones in steeplechasing. Foul riding, or simply incompetent riding, is frequently more of a hazard to horse and jockey than the obstacles themselves.

King explains: 'As long as I have been riding, there have always been a few dirty jockeys who would "do" you whether they had any chance in the race or not. In that, we are no different to any other sport. There are footballers who kick opponents for no gain, fast bowlers who bounce tailenders when the game is won, and so on. You have to be of a certain mentality to behave that way, and I have never understood it.'

'In the course of a season, I will probably be cut up from the outside at least 20 times. Often, it is difficult to tell whether it is deliberate or not. These days, I tend to think the fault is very frequently incompetence rather than malice—but unfortunately, those who are incompetent tend to make a dangerous habit of the practise.'

Put in layman's language, the way to imagine the problem is to run around the inside rails of a racecourse. If someone running on your outer, at similar speed, suddenly accelerated and moved across, you would very probably be forced into, or over, the rails. The tactics can create still more danger at the approach to a jump, where balance and stride are vital.

'For anyone that way inclined, it is so easy to do,' says King. 'You could hurt someone every day of the season if you wanted to. I have seen plenty of villains in my time—and I have seen stacks of riders properly done, with nothing at all they could do about it. It is frequently a personal feud, and some jockeys will come back to the weighing room and want to fight about it there. Others wait for another day, and their own chance to copy the treatment, tit for tat.

'There are occasions when uninvolved jockeys will make it their business to interfere, to sort out the culprit in the weighing-room later. But this happens more often in cases of young jockeys who have ridden dangerously without knowing, or probably caring.

'I have been lucky. I've never been seriously hurt by such riding—but I've lost count of the amount of times blokes have tried. I think of two or three, in particular, who would murder you for practice, even if they were finishing 20th and you were 21st. The race was not complete unless they had put someone in trouble.

'In recent years, I believe deliberately foul riding has become less prevalent—but a jockey is probably more prone to being put in the rails now than ever before. This, to my mind, is through one development—too many lads are being allowed to ride, without enough talent or experience.

'There are maybe twice as many jockeys going round the courses now than when I started riding. Until recently, the youngsters, claiming the four or seven-pound allowance, were still able to collect the full riding fee. But now that the trainers can take half, they are far more enthusiastic about putting up lads to ride. This has contrasting effects. It certainly gives the youngsters greater opportunities and incentives, but it also breeds a complacency among both trainers and jockeys.

'Rides are too easy to give and too easy to get. Which means, over a period of time, that far too many bad riders are allowed to keep a job, primarily because they are saving the trainers' money. All this is compounded by the sudden increase in Opportunity races, which are basically for claimers. I agree with having a certain amount of such races, but with the number on the programmes now, a claimer is becoming known without making any progress as a jockey.

'When there are 16 or 18 young lads going round, the blind are leading the blind. Far more lessons can be learned by the youngsters who ride with more experienced jockeys. Unfortunately, with the system as it is, a good proportion are surviving for two or three seasons, picking up 80 or 100 rides a year, and then fading from the game for ever. In truth, they were never going to be good enough—but the rules allowed them to kid themselves for so long.

'The vast number of young jockeys can only breed incompetence. I maintain that even someone without any great knowledge of racing could watch 20 lads cantering down to the start and identify those who could ride from those who could not. Some look as though they have been thrown at the horse from 20 yards and have sat where they landed.

'Trouble on the course follows automatically. On countless occasions, I have yelled abuse at a rider who has left me pulling to stay alive by cutting across me onto the rails. Yet when I have got back to the weighing-room, he has had no idea what I am complaining about.

'The stewards cannot escape some responsibility, as I feel much of this dangerous riding should be spotted and punished. Too much of the stewards' time appears to be taken up with menial duties, such as supervising the horses leaving the paddock, when jockeys are getting away with crime after crime on the course.

'I would like to see it made a regular practise for stewards to stand on the bends and observe all that goes on there. It happens in flat racing, and jockeys are subsequently stood down for several days with great regularity. I do not accept that jumping should be treated so differently. The excuse is that long distances in heavy ground can produce a good deal of uncontrollable wandering in many horses. That is true. But experienced stewards should be able to differentiate between the whims of jockeys and horses.

'If the villains, and the incompetents, were stood down whenever they were caught "doing" someone, it might just teach them a lesson. Take their wages away for a week and they might think twice before forcing the next one onto the rails.'

It won't help the rider who lost his leg, or the countless others who have been seriously injured, either deliberately, or accidentally. But it might help the next generation.

Whipping

Nothing in racing is more calculated to arouse public anger than whipping. Each year, with the inevitability of Christmas, a flood of mail will hit the mat of newspapers, containing complaints about 'the beasts masquerading as jockeys' who flog their poor horses half to death.

Early in 1980, the Jockey Club decided to play their part in the outrage, and instructed their local stewards to exercise firmer control over excessive use of the whip. As a swift result, two Irishmen were banned for three months after each had offended twice during the Cheltenham Festival, and Andy Turnell, one of the gentlest of riders, was sent before the senior stewards at Portman Square for allegedly over-using his stick on Hill of Slane at both Cheltenham and Aintree.

Turnell was subsequently cleared of all charges. Perhaps significantly, his case was heard after a panel of jockeys, from both flat and jump racing, had met with administrators to discuss the issue which was becoming rapidly more confusing.

Various riders declared that they were afraid to pick up their whip for fear of stewards' reprisals, yet at the same time were wary of dropping their hands on the horse in case they were accused of 'stopping' it.

At the Aintree meeting, Jeff King gave the labouring Pencraig a slap just as the field passed in front of the stands for the first time in Friday's handicap 'chase. His whip connected with some padding behind the horse's saddle and made a resounding crack, like a gunshot. 'I knew it could be heard in the stand,' he said later, 'and I almost hoped the stewards would call me in over it, because a necessary clampdown was becoming a hysterical witch-hunt.'

'Many people outside racing will perhaps see two or three big events on television each year and, without really knowing what they are watching, get very worked up about the apparent amount of whipping. They see jockeys raising their stick high and bringing it down, and perhaps understandably, they assume the horse is taking a terrible beating. In fact, in the vast majority of cases, the horse is not being hit nearly so hard as it might appear.

'Some horses run better for just being shown the stick in the jockey's hand; others benefit from the occasional reminder down the shoulders. Very few horses are actually hurt by the treatment they receive, and it is true to say that most would not run if they were.

'Andy Turnell is a sympathetic rider who has sometimes been accused of being too weak, so it was ironical that he should be the one caught up in this business. Having watched the races involved, I believe that although his whip made contact with Hill of Slane a fair number of times after the last hurdle on each occasion, most of the strikes were applied as backhand taps.

'Unfortunately, certain horses bruise and mark very easily, when in fact they have not been injured at all. Others react the opposite way and can take a concerted beating without any visible effects. Roman Holiday, a great old chaser I rode for many years, often came back from a race with bruises and lumps all down his shoulder, after I had given him no more than a handful of gentle reminders.

'Whipping is undoubtedly a very emotive issue in racing, and there is a school of thought which insists sticks should be completely done away with. I tend to disagree, as I see the application of the whip, in both steering and urging, as one of the skills of a jockey—and there are many around the circuit who are blatantly useless at it.

'The Irishmen, Joe Byrne and Tommy Ryan, incited a public outcry with their displays at Cheltenham. Letters poured into *The Sporting Life* and the other morning papers, and for once I did not think the reaction was too inflated. Both Byrne and Ryan flogged their mounts mercilessly from the last and did nothing to further racing's good name. In Byrne's case, indeed, his treatment of Batista in the Triumph Hurdle probably cost him the race as the horse patently did not respond to such heavy-handed tactics.

'There is certainly a need for a close watch over use of the stick, and strong sentences in certain rare cases. But what the public should realise is that, while some horses go better for a certain amount of whipping and others go better for none at all, very few are physically damaged by their jockeys. If they were, their appetite for racing would diminish overnight and they would be useless in future outings.'

The subject, however, remained newsworthy through the season, being discussed endlessly by television's racing experts and in the press, quite apart from in the weighing-rooms and stewards' rooms of courses around the country.

Arising from the Turnell case, Alan Jarvis, the trainer of Hill of Slane, was also brought before the Portman Square stewards to answer charges that he had induced his jockey to break the rules of racing. The claim was made after Turnell had repeated a parade-ring conversation with Jarvis to the Liverpool stewards, in his own defence.

Jarvis, apparently unhappy with the way Hill of Slane had run at Cheltenham, instructed Turnell to keep him awake, 'even if it means giving him one'. Turnell, with a sardonic reference to the current campaign, had replied: 'I can get three months for that'. Jarvis apparently continued the joke with the comment: 'In that case, I will send you somewhere nice.'

The possibility that the closing remark constituted a bribe seems a remote one, yet it was this line that the Jockey Club pursued. Jarvis angrily took legal advice and threatened to sue for libel, slander and defamation of character, but the whole thing was dropped when he was cleared in the resultant enquiry—attended, incidentally by two television commentators and champion jockey John Francome, all acting as witnesses.

King's reaction to the enquiry into Jarvis was: 'A complete farce. It is naive and nonsensical to construe such a conversation as a bribe, and all it did was bring unwanted and unnecessary publicity to the sport. I have never seen or heard of any jump jockey being offered a bribe—unless you count a tip from the owner as such—and the only similar case in my memory was that concerning John Francome and the bookmaker John Banks.'

The entire affair, however, reverted to the subject of whipping and I had discovered that any conversation on this issue between a group of jump jockeys was likely to include two names—Jonjo O'Neill and Lester Piggott. O'Neill was thought by some of his colleagues to be whip-happy; Piggott was accused of it almost unanimously.

But as King concludes: 'Lester sometimes looks as though he is cracking them like a machine-gun. But still he gets them home—and I would estimate that a fair number of his big winners would not have got there if he had not used such tactics.'

TOP: One of the less attractive faces of racing – Ayr on a wet one.

ABOVE: With all the mud slung on the subject of whipping, an oddly apt picture of Irishman Tommy Ryan, immediately after the strongarm display at Cheltenham which earned him a three-month ban.

147

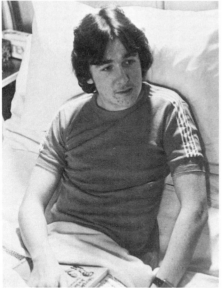

TOP: A memorable moment in King's career. Big Ben, outjumped, unships Tommy Carmody and Drusus goes on to win the State Express Young Chasers' Final at Cheltenham, giving King his 700th winner.

ABOVE: Baffled, bewildered and puzzling over a life which one fall had dreadfully distorted, Jonathan Haynes talks from his Sheffield hospital bed.

148

Doping

Fifteen days after the event, the 1980 Cheltenham Gold Cup was reduced to a fiasco when a dope test of the winning horse, Tied Cottage, proved positive. Yet, despite the inevitable decision to disqualify the 'drugged' animal and award the race to Master Smudge, there had almost certainly been no intent on the part of Tied Cottage's trainer.

The substance theobromine was discovered in urine samples taken from Tied Cottage, and two other horses—all three were Irish-trained. But although proof is unlikely to be produced, the overwhelming probability is that the dope was contained in the horses' feed.

Routine tests are made on every course, and after every race, by a team of travelling specialists. At Cheltenham, for instance, 12 tests were taken on each of the three days. The remaining 33 at the meeting were all negative.

When a positive result is obtained, details are transferred to the Jockey Club, who set their sleuths to work. Racecourse Security Services is the game's detective force, with a string of investigators paid to look into alleged or potential crooked practices, of which doping is only one. Another, still more sensational and unusual, involves the running of 'ringers'—horses who are not who they are supposed to be. One such case occurred at Newton Abbot in 1978 and, after scrupulous investigations by the security services, trainer John Bowles was given an 18-month suspended prison sentence and fined £1,500, with a further £1,500 costs, at Exeter Crown Court.

Doping, however, has become virtually extinct as a deliberate attempt to win, or sometimes lose a race, since the introduction of such stringent tests.

Jeff King explains: 'Almost all winners are tested, and usually another horse in each race, chosen at random. Against such odds, there seems no point in doping and I cannot believe much of it goes on these days. The exceptions are the accidental cases, when a trainer uses nuts in the horses' feed which contain too much of a certain substance.'

'Even then, I doubt very much whether a race would be affected at all—and certainly, in Tied Cottage's case, there is no reason to suspect he would not have won without the drug. Only old, arthritic horses can have their running improved by certain painkilling drugs, illegal in Britain but allowed in America, where horses using such drugs are marked on the racecard.

'There have certainly been cases of horses being doped to lose races, but this has generally been the work of gangsters breaking into yards to administer the dope. Suspicion has occasionally fallen on bookmakers in such incidents.

'When I was riding for Bob Turnell, his stables were done at least twice, but on both occasions, too much of the dope was given. A horse called The Finn, a light-framed animal, was due to run in the

Champion Hurdle at Cheltenham one year, and I was to ride him. Two days before the race, I rode him at work, and he could not even walk up the road. For ten minutes or so, as the horse staggered drunkenly, I thought he was ill from natural causes, but it was not long before we discovered the truth. He missed the race, which was probably not the gang's intention at all.

'If a horse is given a correct dose of a drug and remains well enough to go to post for a race, it could be that nobody ever discovers he has been doped. I am quite sure this has happened on any number of occasions over the years. Just because a horse has run badly, there is no reason to suspect foul play. They are not machines, after all.

'But in the great majority of cases, the jockey of a drugged horse would know what had happened going down to the start, if not before.

'Doping may well have been a reasonably common practice before the days of daily tests. But I very much doubt if it thrives now.'

King's views were probably those of Racecourse Security Services, too. But such faith would not help the connections of Tied Cottage, who had just lost £36,000 and untold glory—all for a new nuts.

14 Triumph and tragedy

All through the season, Doddington Park had been one of King's favourite rides. One of his most successful, too, providing three of his modest winning tally. And all season, the horse had been aimed at the final of the State Express Young Steeplechasers' event, scheduled for Cheltenham on April 10.

A week before the race came the news that Drusus was declared for the same event. King, having taken a retainer to ride the horse, had no choice and prepared to tell Nick Gaselee, trainer of Doddington Park, that he would need a different jockey.

Privately, King considered that Drusus would probably win a straight race between the two, in ideal conditions, but this was still another example of the unhappy clashes which so often beset jockeys. Regularly during the season, King seemed either to have two possible rides in a race, or none at all.

This time, however, he was spared the possibility of any distressing ironies. Doddington Park unshipped his rider while in training work and sustained an injury serious enough to eliminate him from the race. King had not even had time to talk to Gaselee. Omen or not, it was a stroke of fortune which certainly helped bring King his most valuable, and best-received victory of the season.

On the dazzlingly sunny morning of the race, almost every press tipster opted for Drusus, and by the time the tapes went up, the horse had been backed to odds-on. Not that it would concern King, who has no time for the theory that a long-priced winner is a bigger thrill than a favourite. 'The betting generally reflects the horses' quality fairly faithfully,' he says, 'and the best sensation I know is to ride a top-class horse at speed over fences. So it follows that I enjoy winning on favourites more than on outsiders.'

Cheltenham was strikingly picturesque in the spring sunshine, the Cotswolds a compelling backdrop to a scene which seemed to grow greener as you watched. But it was a far cry from the rumbustious crush of the Festival meeting, just four weeks earlier. One could stroll around the course without being barged by an intoxicated punter every five yards. A bet could be placed without a 20-minute queue, a beer bought without claustrophobic scrummaging and clumsy spilling. Even the hot dogs and hamburger counter, with its pretentious 'Bill of Fare' notice above the tomato ketchup, looked more inviting.

Drusus trotted keenly around the paddock, lifting up his feet as if impatient to be on with the race. King, conversely, lagged behind most of his rival jockeys. He paused to sign an autograph on his stroll from the weighing-room and looked calm and unconcerned. Nothing new, after all—just a rather more pressing assignment than it might have been in a more successful season.

He sent Drusus to the front of the field early in the race and was never out of the first two. Perhaps still mentally wary from his recent unhappy experiences, however, Drusus jumped without the freedom and conviction of which he is capable. Three fences from home, Tommy Carmody's mount Big Ben approached the front with an ominously powerful challenge. King summoned Drusus for the vital effort, stood off yards from the jump and achieved a spectacular leap. It would conceivably have gained Drusus a length even if Big Ben had survived. As it was, striving to match the take-off, he crashed into the fence and deposited Carmody on the turf, leaving King to win as he pleased.

Polite applause from the crowd gathered around the unsaddling enclosure greeted King and Drusus. King touched his cap in the time-honoured fashion, dismounted, shared a few words with trainer Rimell and the horse's effusively delighted owner Bob Brown and disappeared into the weighing-room for the rush to change for his next ride.

It was King's first winner in almost seven weeks. One of the longest waits of his career for one of the most significant successes. For this was his 700th win, a figure achieved by only six jockeys in steeplechasing history and only two—Ron Barry and Bob Davies—who are still riding.

The press were fulsome in their praise. *The Times* described his riding of Drusus as 'inspired'; *The Sporting Life* called it 'brilliant'. *The Daily Express* told its readers that Jeff 'has not had the mounts this season that his outstanding talents deserve'; the *Sporting Chronicle* wrote of 'his magnificent career'.

King, however, would not have spent the following morning buying all the papers and poring gloatingly over such reviews. After a night spent in his favourite local pubs, drinking halves of bitter, digesting an enormous plate of steak and chips and chalking for a friends' darts match, he had his usual six hours sleep before riding out his horses and meditating on his tractor. His concession to the press enthusiasm would have been, quite without malice, to excuse their writers for knowing so little about the game.

Jon Haynes
On Saturday 19 April, Jeff King's only booked ride at the Worcester

meeting, a modest novice, was withdrawn before racing. King instead took his family off for a weekend with friends and may easily have pondered wearily over the season now drawing into its final month.

Eight months it had been running. Eight months in which King had driven many thousands of miles, and ridden several hundred. Yet those eight months had produced just 17 winners, and his final tally seemed sure to be his lowest since 1963.

It seemed a very long time since that mid-November success on Doddington Park in the cold and damp of Chepstow, where this account started out. Since then, in fact, King had won on just 11 of 158 mounts. Thirty-two others had been placed in the first three and, surprisingly, only five had fallen.

If nothing else, King had survived the majority of the season without serious injury, which was more than could be said for many among his colleagues. On April 19, for instance, although he doubtless did not realise it, 20-year-old Jonathan Haynes was spending his 100th day in hospital.

Haynes' tragic accident in the seller at Southwell during a nondescript January meeting, had caused tremors through the racing world. A second enquiry, reconvened after pressure from various quarters, had just announced their findings. They had declared that Haynes' regrettable injuries could not conceivably have been caused, or even aggravated, by the treatment he received.

So that was that. Funds had been set up, it is true, and Haynes would receive some sort of aid to start him in another career. Though just what he could do was not yet clear. The boy who had lived for horses, loved the racing game more than anything on earth, and never imagined the day when he would have to desert it, was destined to see the rest of his life from a wheelchair. A jump jockey no more.

The highlight of Jon Haynes' 100th day in hospital was an attempt to walk five yards. Not far, maybe, but for one whose life had shuddered to a stop like a stalled car, those five yards of movement were a consuming ambition.

His boyish face set grimly, somewhere between determination and desperation, Haynes tottered those few paces with human support hovering anxiously on each side. His withered and useless legs, which less than four months earlier had driven home his first National Hunt winner, were clamped in calipers for the marathon. It will never be much better. Against himself, Haynes makes a joke. 'I might be able to walk a quarter of a mile in these one day. But it will take me at least four hours.'

As hospitals go, Lodge Moor is almost attractive. I had driven through Sheffield, past vast steelworks, endless banks of terraced houses packed tighter than a rugby league scrum and through a claustrophobic town centre where the pervading smell was overcooked cabbage. But once away from the smoke, into the hazy sunshine of the April afternoon, the moors rolled enticingly into the distance. A golf course borders Lodge Moor Hospital, not that it will ever benefit Jon Haynes now.

The hospital buildings were elderly but smart, designed in symmetrical blocks with a connecting maze of corridors. The antiseptic smell which haunts the minds of many with bad memories of hospitals, was surprisingly subdued, and there was no evidence of the cracked ceilings and grubby walls suffered by the places of my experience.

At the entrance to Ward South 3, an orderly was washing the floor. Jon was not in his bed, she told me. 'He can get about now, you know.' She pointed me to the visitors' lounge, a few doors down, and there I found him, sitting in his wheelchair dressed in a red, Liverpool Football Club tracksuit, a heavy gold medallion round his neck pointing almost to the mark across his chest where his movement and feeling came to an abrupt end.

Sitting quietly with him was a tall girl with long, blond hair. His girlfriend of three years, she had endured as much of a shock as anyone. Every visiting day, she travelled faithfully from the Staffordshire village where she lived. She had met Jon there, in his time as apprentice to trainer Reg Hollinshead. 'He was always a daredevil, a real character,' she said. 'The neighbours used to complain about him because he made such a noise in his car. He used to chase the lads around the yard in it, blasting the horn. Mind you, he never used to talk as much then.'

There is certainly none of the silent martyr in Haynes. In almost two hours, he paused only to be prompted onto a new subject or, more regularly, to concentrate on trying to halt the twitching spasms which afflicted his right leg. 'It would do this all day if I allowed it,' he apologised as the knee throbbed like an outboard motor. He can stop it only by pressing hard on the thigh for about 30 seconds. 'The feeling has gone, like, but there are still some nerves alive in there somewhere. Often, when I am trying to lift myself onto the bed, the legs keep jumping off.'

The worst of the pain, he explained, had subsided within three weeks of the accident. All that was left was an occasional ache and a constant sense of nothingness masquerading as limbs.

Haynes' life in Lodge Moor was regimented, the routine adhered to on all but visiting days when the afternoons were free. He was woken at 6.30 a.m., breakfast at 7.00 a.m. and had a bath soon afterwards. Much of the morning was occupied by an individual programme of physiotherapy in the hospital gym, and lunch was served at 12.00 p.m.

For an hour each afternoon, Haynes reported for OT—occupational therapy—and it was here that he was finding the bricks to build a new future. 'I am learning to type,' he explained, 'and doing woodwork so that I can make things I will need when I get out.'

After another physio session between 3.00 and 4.30 p.m., those who felt up to it played a bizarre game of basketball, in wheelchairs, for an hour. 'It helps to get the balance back, but there are plenty of collisions, with blokes being knocked out of their chairs and suchlike.'

Tea is at 5.30 p.m., and the evening then stretches ahead. Haynes sometimes watched television, or listened to the radio. More often, he would read *The Sporting Life* and the *Timeform* book which an owner had given him. '*The Life* is my bible. I can't wait for it to arrive every morning. It's the only way I have to keep in touch with what's going on. I watch all the racing on television too, of course, but that is sometimes a bit painful. I miss it like hell, but it is still good to see my mates in action.'

His 'mates' and colleagues were being good to Haynes. Each jockey was donating one riding fee to a fund set up for him; raffles and auctions were being organised; functions were being arranged; an old friend who had turned pro as a boxer was giving him his next fight purse; jobs, to somehow keep him connected with the sport, were being invented.

As ever, the jockeys were closing ranks to protect and support one of their own. The sympathy for his plight was intense, the concern over the circumstances of his injuries universal. Two separate inquiries into the incident had been held by the Jockey Club, but they finally declared, with some regret, that Haynes must have been suffering from 'cruel tricks of the memory' to state that he had been pulled from beneath his dead horse and that he had then waited almost three hours for hospital treatment.

They maintained that, although facilities on the fateful Southwell course left something to be desired in certain respects—there were no signal flags on the fence where the accident occured, and the handles of the stretcher provided did not extend, to name two such misgivings—Jon's 'appalling injuries were not compounded by the treatment he received'.

Following the first inquiry, the Jockey Club had said they were satisfied that all was in order. They re-opened investigations only after representations from Haynes' boss, Jimmy Harris, and a letter from Haynes himself, demanding to know why he had not been consulted. 'I wrote it lying flat on my back in bed,' he recalls, 'and had to apologise for the handwriting.'

The main points of contention surrounded Haynes' dogmatic assertions that the fence-minder had dragged his right leg—the one which still continually twitched—from beneath the hind quarters of his mount, Shiny Step before putting him more upright, and that it had taken from 2 p.m., until around 4.30 p.m. for the Newark Hospital staff to x-ray his back.

Haynes's first claim was discounted, seemingly because the Jockey Club maintained that the fence-minder was unlikely to have been physically capable of the act. He was 75.

His second claim was rebuffed by evidence from hospital staff and independent witnesses, and the enquiry concluded that Haynes was 'at best only semi-conscious at the course and in no condition to recall the circumstances in any detail.'

What Haynes did not tell the committee of enquiry is that, while waiting for treatment at Newark Hospital, he was crying out in pain. A nurse, he says, approached with some annoyance and told him that he shouldn't be making any noise because he only had rib injuries. She added a slap round the face. On learning how serious Haynes' injuries in fact were, the nurse wrote to apologise to him, and he still has the letter.

Whatever the true facts behind the episode—and, although I was at Southwell that day, I was totally unaware of the drama being enacted—all the evidence merely adds weight to the theory of a majority of jockeys that the safety precautions provided for them are laughable.

Stories abound of alarming incidents after falls, both in the medical room and the hospitals afterwards. Jeff King tells the tale of Bill Shoemark, now in a livery business on King's land, suffering a bad case of concussion from a fall during his jockey days. 'Bill was so bad he was in cloud cuckoo land. Yet when they got him to the casualty department of a hospital, they refused to treat him, claiming he was drunk!'

King himself believes much of the trouble is that the voluntary St John's Ambulance men, of which there are six on most courses, generally have little or no knowledge of racing, or racing injuries. 'When I broke my leg at Wetherby,' he recalls, 'one of them tried to drag me off the track immediately. Apart from the fact that it could have done nothing but harm, there was no point in moving me because it would be another three minutes before the field passed that point again ... something he was totally unaware of.'

John Francome is in favour of a jockeys' campaign for more professional medical care on ALL racecourses, and draws a parallel with the sport of motor-racing. 'Tell the Grand Prix drivers that they were going around Monza with a few St Johns Ambulance men to look after them, and there would be no race,' he says with forceful logic.

Haynes would also welcome such action. Although nothing can be done to put the clock back on his behalf, it might conceivably help to prevent another such dreadful accident.

Meanwhile, all he can do is relish the memories of his own brief, yet promising career in the racing business, a career which began in unorthodox, if romantic fashion when he quit school at the age of $13^1/_2$.

'I was a terrible scholar, and I know I am not the brightest now. I used to skive all through my schooldays, mainly to be with horses, and when I did go to school I hated it because there was so much catching up to be done. I got myself into awful trouble, regular like, but I don't regret anything I have done.'

Born in Morecambe, where his family still live, Jon was one of two children for a man whose frustrated ambition had been to be a jockey. Due to that, Jon was given every encouragement, and soon needed no more. At the age of 11, while riding at Hickstead on the show-jumping pony his father had bought for him, he approached David Mould to ask for an opening into the racing world. Mould suggested young Haynes contacted him again 'when he was old enough'. He did, two years later, and Mould kept his word, helping him into Frenchie Nicholson's training yard, much renowned as a jockeys' academy.

'The school governors came round to our house, but my Dad told them I had left home and he didn't know where I had gone. He was good like that, because he wanted me to get on.'

Haynes stayed with Nicholson for two years. 'And that was two years start on every other kid coming into the job at 16,' he points out. 'I was lucky to get the experience so early.' From there, he joined Reg Hollinshead at Upper Longdon, and was sent back to school for two afternoons a week. 'I was supposed to go every day, actually, but that was enough. It got me my leaving certificate and meant everything was above board.'

For more than three years, Haynes grew up at Hollinshead's yard. He rode on the flat for the first time, finishing sixth at Thirsk—'I reckon I would have won but the horse broke down a furlong out ... but everyone says that about their first ride, don't they?'—and collected his debut winner on Red Dawn at Hamilton Park. But, like many other jump jockeys who have passed through the other half of the game, he never settled on the flat.

'It came natural to me to see the stride of a horse up to a fence, through having been showjumping. I always wanted to go jumping, and I was really too tall for the flat anyway, so when I began to put on weight, I wasn't a bit disappointed. In fact I started eating like a pig, just to make sure there was no going back. I never felt right on the flat, somehow, and there were even times when I was disillusioned with the jockey's existence then. But my first ride over hurdles changed it all. I never realised just how great racing was until that day—taking jumps at speed must be the greatest sensation there is.'

It was around this time that Haynes joined Jimmy Harris's stable at Melton Mowbray, producing the startling irony of his current situation. For Haynes, too, is a paraplegic, another victim of a steeplechasing fall. He operates his training business from a wheelchair, managing his life supremely well and concealing the frustrations he must inevitably harbour.

Haynes recalls: 'I used to get very tired after my first few rides over jumps, and Jim would make me go out running every evening to get fitter. Often, I was slumped in a chair after a day's work and the last thing I wanted was to slog round the lanes. But Jim was insistent. He used to say: "If I had legs, I would run." It sounds strange now, doesn't it?

'I had read books and articles about jockeys getting hurt badly, and of course Jim used to tell me about his accident. But none of it seemed very significant. I mean, you never think it will happen to you.

'This was my first serious fall, you know. I'd come off before, of course, but I had never been hurt. A broken leg, or broken collarbone maybe—I could have handled all that, and it would at least have given me the opportunity to sit back and think whether the life was worth all the risks. I never got that second chance.'

It would take the iciest of cynics to condemn Haynes if he sometimes wallows in self pity. Throughout those 100 days in hospital there had been too much time to think of what might have been. He had never enjoyed a full night's sleep, because he had to be turned every two hours. He had never enjoyed peace of mind through a day, because his bible *The Sporting Life* brought his losses flooding back.

'I had just been starting to go well when this happened. It takes time to get going in this game, but I felt things were turning my way. On Boxing Day at Market Rasen, I came to the last just edging ahead and thought I was in for my first jumping winner. But the horse unseated me. I only had to wait five more days, though. New Years Eve it was, my winner. My only one, as things turned out. But in the three days before my accident, I had five outside rides. People were noticing me.'

'I was small compared to most jump jockeys, which meant I found it easier to really get down over the horse and ride a finish. My flat rides had helped there, too. And I had plenty of dare—I didn't mind taking a bit of a gamble at a fence. I have always been daft since schooldays. It was always me who took the dares and got into trouble.'

On the day that Haynes took his final racing risk, Jimmy Harris arranged to collect him from hospital at 5.00 p.m., unaware of the severity of his injuries. As Haynes said: 'At first I just felt as if my chest was crushed, so everyone thought it must be my ribs that had gone.'

Harris and his wife arrived on time, just as Haynes was settling into his longest stay in bed. 'Jim said he'd come to take me home. I told him I wasn't going anywhere because I'd broken my back. He just stood and looked at me as if he couldn't believe it, and I'm told his wife ran out crying. I was still too shocked to notice much.'

'It must have brought back horrible memories to Jim and his wife, and for quite a while, I know he couldn't face me. He wanted to come to the hospital more, but I think he hated seeing me in this state, just like he'd been years ago.'

Haynes' parents were as badly affected as one would expect with the knowledge that his mother is an invalid with a heart condition and his father, a power station chief foreman, had set his heart on Jon achieving the success as a jockey which he himself had always yearned.

'My mother took it better than I'd expected, because she had always worried about me riding anyway. But Dad was heartbroken. He had taken me around the yards and got me into racing. I think it was his greatest wish that I should do well. He got himself in such a state when he visited that he once told me he wouldn't come again. I think he kept believing that I would get up and walk, until the night before the Grand National when he came in just as I was struggling to get on the bed, with my legs jumping off. He saw me in that mess and said to a nurse: "He is never going to move again, is he". He stayed that night, and was back next morning. He's been alright ever since.'

Only occasionally during the two hours that we talked did Haynes look emotional. Now and again, he would wipe his sleeve across his brow, sweeping his dark curls out of his eyes or maybe repelling an imminent tear. Yet when he talked of his future, or what was left of it, he had quite patently come to terms with his predicament.

'I have accepted it, mainly because I have seen Jim get on. I don't expect to be able to train but I am determined to stay in racing. Brough Scott came in to see me, and told me I must try to better myself. That's why I am learning to type. When I get out, and I'm allowed to work, I will take some college classes and then just hope that someone in the sport will employ me.

'These six years I have spent working should just have been the start of my life, shouldn't it. Well, perhaps I've got to start again now. But racing is all I know. I want to stay connected with horses as closely as I can, but if it comes to it, I will work in a betting shop just to stay involved.

'I don't want to be forgotten in racing, you see. I may not have done much, but I would like to think people will remember me as a jump jockey.'

ACKNOWLEDGEMENTS

The author and publishers would like to thank the following for supplying the photographs :
Bespix, pages 29 and 55; E. C. Byrne, title page; Gerry Cranham for the back and front jacket photographs and those on pages 39, 67, 68, 83, 84, 103, 121, 133 and 147 top and bottom; Provincial Press Agency, page 16; Alec Russell, pages 106, 122 and 148; Selwyn Photos for the frontispiece and pages 15, 29, 30/31, 32, 40, 56, 104/105, 106, 134 and 148; Sport and General Press Agency, pages 13 and 14/15,